Girl Dad

Navigating Fatherhood With Daughters

David Hall

Contents

Introduction

Fatherhood is more than someone calling you "dad" or teaching someone how to do the "manly" things in life like changing a car's brake pads or playing catch with a baseball and glove. Fatherhood is a lifelong commitment. It's a noble, hard, and worthwhile endeavor to stay present as much as possible for your children when the weight of the world is on your shoulders to provide shelter, sustenance, and support.

Anyone can be a "dad" in the biological sense, but being a father denotes dedication, putting your phone down, and leaving that work email unread to watch your daughter turn one more cartwheel—and to see one more play or pageant. Even listening to an ear-splitting rendition of "Mary Had a Little Lamb" on recorder and producing the appropriate, emphatic round of applause afterward means you're doing it right—because you're there, and your child notices.

Being a "girl dad" takes even more effort and dedication because you're responsible for getting this right—right off the bat. The moment you hold your tiny human in your hands, you have her heart. She'll look up to you like you're her story-book prince, indomitable superhero. You'll need to do all the things you said you would and have the forethought to provide even more—because, sadly, if you don't she'll be more likely to spend the rest of her adult life looking for someone who does. And he, more often than not, will *not* have her best interests in mind; he'll be putting himself first.

But never fear! There is always time to swoop in and repair or remake your presence in your daughter's life no matter how young or old either of you may be. She'll always be your daughter, just like you'll always be her dad. So, no matter what transpired between your child's birth to now, it's equally vital to understand your role as the father of a daughter.

You don't want to miss even a single second, if you can help it, because infancy, toddlerhood, the school years, young adult-hood, college, marriage, relationships, jobs, and moving out as an adult: It all goes by too quickly even if it feels like you'll never catch a wink of sleep because you've just started your journey into fatherhood.

Parenthood can be exhausting. Do your best to stay present, and stay awake. This book will give you the best tips on just how to be the best "girl dad" you can be whatever your daugh-ter's interests or present age. Any girl dad could benefit from reading this book. Congratulations to you throughout it all. You're already doing an awesome job!

The Importance of Being a Girl Dad

Never underestimate the incredible power you have as a father to shape, to protect, and to instill the utmost confidence in your children. Your very presence (putting down your phone or other distraction to engage with your children) deeply reduces the likelihood of your children acquiring an eating disorder, becoming pregnant as a teen, attempting suicide, experiencing major depression and anxiety, and experimenting with drugs, alcohol, nicotine, and other harmful substances.

You alone have the power to provide the perfect example of what a mature, respectful, reciprocal relationship should look like and how it should work by doing your very best to maintain this kind of relationship with your daughter's mother. Whether you are married, divorced, or somewhere complicated in between: It's still your responsibility to be respectful whenever your daughter can view or hear what you say, how you feel, and if you disagree with her mother.

Your daughter loves her mother, the same as she loves you. Even if you don't get along with this person who gave birth and is doing her best to raise your child with you, the best thing you can do for your children is to treat this relationship as professionally as possible. Showing respect at every turn will instill this value in your child, too. She will respect herself and gain confidence because her home life will not cause constant anxiety she is forced to battle internally. Even if her home is divided between mom and dad, your daughter won't have to scramble to pick up yours or her mother's pieces after needless arguments.

This seems simple, or impossible, but it truly will make or break your daughter and her future relationships. Trust within a family, like unconditional love, goes such a long way to keeping your daughter safe from predators who would mistreat her when all she wants is to feel safe and to believe that there are good people out there.

You may not always be able to count on her mother to do the same, but you can always choose how you handle a heated

Introduction

situation. Go for a walk to cool off, but never permanently walk away from your child. Her relationship with you should be separate from the relationship you have with others, and even with your child's mother no matter how complicated or impossible your relationship—or lack thereof—may be.

It's going to sound cruel, but it is serious—of the utmost importance that you understand: Most of what you need to keep your daughter safe and out of the crosshairs of a predator's sights is to keep her whole. Don't make her search for the broken, missing pieces you left on your desk at work or in your phone during family time. Don't make her choose sides or a favorite parent because the only person who loses is your daughter.

Get over yourself, your relationship hang-ups and insecurities, and put your little girl first. She is nothing like all the other women you've ever known before, unless you let your careless actions turn her into that. Every broken woman used to be bright and shiny before she was hurt by someone she believed in.

If your daughter asks you to play with dolls with her, do it. If she's playing dress-up or make believe, you should throw everything you've got into your valiant prince or fierce dragon performance. Check under the bed twice for any monsters she fears and check her phone messages, SnapChat, Instagram, and social media for monsters there, too, when she gets to be a preteen.

Be on the frontlines in her army every opportunity you get, ready to take a bullet for this precious child. Swallow your pride if you can't reach an agreeable solution with her mother if you're separated or going through a rough time together. Do anything and everything you can to be there, to show up at events—in the front row, camera ready. Be ready to move any argument to a lower, more civilized tone or out of earshot altogether so that your daughter never falters in knowing that both of her parents have her back at a moment's notice. Work together as best you can.

Put your daughter first in every instance and you will be rewarded with a rich, healthy, trusting relationship with a little girl who grows into a confident woman who realizes her worth. She can crack, then shatter any glass ceiling and won't risk settling for less than her daddy gave her.

Unique Rewards of Being a Girl Dad

As the father of a female child, you have the unique role, responsibility, and right to take pride in how successful your daughter is throughout her entire childhood and beyond. The amount of time you pour into your relationship will be the deciding factor between a solid foundation she can fall back on when times get tough as an adult or if she falls through the cracks time and time again if you were not there for the tears, the heartache, the academic pressure, and the personal problems that always arise whenever a child is trying to grow and then stretch their wings.

It is a heady mix of good and bad, as all meaningful things are. Your daughter needs you in her life when she is young, but it's how you handle highly emotional, deeply difficult situations with her as she grows that will determine if she *wants* you in her life when she's an adult.

Put in the effort now and your rewards will be multitudinous. She will bless you with her personal wisdom, her inside jokes, her successes, the pieces of her heart when they need repaired, and by her presence in your life as you age, too. One day, she may even bless you with an equally important role of being a grandfather to her children. If she entrusts you with the tiny humans she's invested so dearly in, you know you've done it all right. Keep up the good work, even though it's sometimes hard work. If you follow her lead, listen to her sincerely, she will be there for you as you were for her.

Throughout this book, you will find tips on how to make the most of your time as a "girl dad." You may have been a man, husband, partner, or "boy dad" before, but now that you are in charge of being the most prominent force for how your daughter will form her attachments in her lifetime, it's a game changer. Wherever your little girl falls in the birth order, make sure to tell her sincerely and often how much joy she brings into your life.

Enjoy every sweet moment, relish this time with your little girl. She will only be so small and helpless for a short period of time before she finds her footing and unsure toddling turns into your having to run to try to catch up to her. Try, try again, and keep trying to be worthy of being part of her world. Back off when she says she needs space, but never quit completely.

You are irreplaceable. But you are also just a human, flawed and full of challenges in your own life just like everyone else. Don't let these dark parts of being an adult infiltrate your relationship with your daughter. This book will show you ways to accomplish being a successful "girl dad," to help you manage life's stresses so that you and your daughter can enjoy a less tense, more lighthearted way of coexisting.

The goal should be that at the end of every interaction, no matter how old your daughter is, that she knows every single day how much you love and appreciate her just the way she is. You may need to push parts of your upbringing, opinions, and notions aside in order to do so, but that is the ultimate objective. You want to know that she loves and appreciates you just the same. That your role in her life has been invaluable and that if she'd had the choice to choose who her father had been, she'd have chosen you without hesitation every single time. That is the magic of being a "girl dad." So let's begin.

Chapter 1
Understanding Your Daughter's World

Like *The Little Mermaid* who just wanted to be part of "their" world, it's imperative you try to do what King Triton did not: Make a valiant effort to understand your daughter's world. It's much different than yours or anything you've ever been part of before.

There are monsters made of more than dust bunnies beneath her bed. There are temptations to dabble in the dangerous pitfalls that hide behind well-dressed college junior facades and promising office parties. And there are fiends disguised as friends who will lead her down the path to the dark side. She will also battle herself, what she sees staring back in the mirror and she'll beat herself up if she fails or doesn't "fit in."

You need to take on the role of letting her discover herself, who she is comfortable being within her own skin, while being ready at a moment's notice to catch her when she falls. You don't want to miss a single step in her development, but you also don't want to smother her to the point that she doesn't realize she can stand on her own two feet.

It's similar to how your helpless infant learned to walk on her own. She builds core muscles herself, gradually over time, but still needs your assistance to steady her vertical endeavor to stand on her own before she can successfully walk.

So don't burn down her underwater grotto in the false hopes that she won't defy your demands; if you listen with an open heart instead of acting out of rash judgment, you'll be part of her world as someone she can trust and rely on in times of trouble. By dismissing her dreams, you would also be severing her growing confidence in herself and her trust in you. She can't confide in someone who will tear her down.

Stay mindful of your choice in words, too. If she's growing too tall to carry anymore, refrain from using the phrase, "You're getting *too big* to pick up." This can imply that she's getting too "heavy" and she may begin to struggle with self-image, weight, and eating enough food to maintain a healthy weight so that she can grow to her full potential. A safe way to say this is that she's growing up and can walk on her own now.

Choose your words, actions, and level of involvement from your daughter's viewpoint—someone who is just beginning their relationship with food, the world outside her front door, and with society and her peers. She's discovering what makes her feel safe so you want to be part of that instead of contributing to any doubts she may have acquired through her time at school or witnessing how the world treats outsiders.

Get Involved in Each of Your Daughter's "Eras"

Is it princesses, superheroes, trucks, tea parties, bugs and rocks, art, or ballet that get your daughter interested? Whatever she is drawn to to express her creativity, follow it with abandon. Even if her hobbies change like the seasons, try to be as enthusiastically supportive as you can. She's trying to discover the best, most joyful way to express herself.

Try to spend one-on-one time with your daughter doing the things that she likes. Then flip the script. Set aside an additional one-on-one session when she can enjoy something with you that you like to do. Play a video game together, let her watch you play, cook one of your favorite dishes or a recipe that was handed down to you from another family member. Let her get to know you, and you should, in turn, spend the same amount of effort and time to get to know her as she grows.

Who your daughter seems to be when she's little may change with experience, exposure to a variety of other exquisite opportunities, cultures, and ways of existing that the real world has to offer. She will form her own opinions when challenged with new information than you've likely been exposed to. This doesn't mean you are wrong or that she's always right. Nothing in life is so black and white or is always so strictly binary. There is an infinite spectrum of existence of shades of gray that exist between these two polar ideas of "wrong" and "right."

You and your daughter will evolve as you both age. Your viewpoints might change, your personalities and the way you dress might also adapt to external influences. The constant attribute of your relationship should be that you would still rather maintain an amicable relationship with each other than reduce your interactions to tense family gatherings, obligatory holiday parties where you only spend as much time together as necessity dictates.

These every-other-weekend types of interactions will not keep your relationship healthy. A single breath of fresh air every other month doesn't keep living organisms alive. If tensions in your interactions become stifling, try to identify *why*. When did your little girl start to let you down or when did you?

Throughout her childhood, your daughter lived under your rules if she lived under your roof. She would have tested your boundaries in using shaving cream as paint and again, as a teen, trying to stay out past curfew. Every child tries to push the limits, this is how they gauge how much they are loved.

But if restrictions are too tight or too loose, the child spirals out of control and begins to dabble in the dangers of adult life. You'll want to set realistic expectations for what you expect in regard to dating, curfew, responsibilities, grades, maintaining the cleanliness of her room, driving, using illegal substances, and how she gets to and from any sports practices. To foster respect for herself, you need to show her that you respect her.

When she was little, your daughter's only worries were limited to the basics like fun, toys, and staying healthy, fed, clean, and loved. Her world gets bigger in elementary, then even bigger again in middle school, and can be immensely overwhelming in high school. There are more people who have the potential to influence your daughter for better or worse as time goes on.

Do your very best to love her, to *show* her how much you love her, keep consistent boundaries in place to protect her, and help her see why those boundaries are necessary to help her learn what is safe and what could end in disaster. You only want to keep her safe. Explain with sincerity that you don't want to keep her locked away. You cannot be selfish like that.

Your goal is to help your daughter survive anything that you aren't able to shield her from and give her the skills she needs to cope when anything breaks through her armor. Tell her that she's the most important person in your life. Tell her often how much you love her regardless of how old she gets or how silly you feel expressing such deep emotion.

The words you choose to surround your daughter with will harden to keep the bullies at bay and protect her with the way they lift her up, help her shine. Any abrasive aggression will leave her waterlogged, heavy with harshness seeping through the cracks left by any vicious vitriol she's caught in the crossfire by if you're constantly arguing with your partner and especially if it's directed at her. She will live her life in hopes that she won't let you down, but she will be lost in the process if you don't make amends for it now.

She should be loved unconditionally for who she is, not for who you want her to be or who you thought she had been. The beauty of growing up is how many versions of ourselves we shed like caterpillar casings until we emerge as our truest selves. She may look totally transformed or seem the same but behave in ways you don't understand.

Love your daughter in all her eras. Ask earnest questions framed to help you understand and get to know your daughter again and again. Talking and listening are the only ways to truly invest enough effort and show her that you care.

Social and Cultural Pressures Facing Young Girls Today

The 21st century is no exception when it comes to adversity facing females of all ages. There has been progress over the course of several centuries of work, but it isn't enough. Your daughter will still be bombarded with images in advertising that tell her she should be skinnier, prettier, and more attractive. She will still earn less money than if she had been born a boy doing the same job. Society will continually expect more from her while simultaneously telling her that she needs to do more, do it better.

You should be prepared, as her father, to reinforce the opposite —that she is capable, she is worthy, she is "good enough," and that she is loved unconditionally regardless of the results she produces because she's amazing however she chooses to dress, to exist, and to pursue her dreams.

If she wants to play sports, she will be told she isn't as good as the boys who perform the same feats. Take the example of the WNBA versus the NBA: The size of the basketball is smaller for the women who play the same sport. But, that's not the worst of it. To play for the women's team, a person must be over 22 years old instead of being only 19 years old for the NBA, all-male team (Janvrin, 2023). Even when the basketball is moved down the same kind of court and thrown into the same net, the difference in who passes the ball to get it in the hoop determines the worth equated to each player.

While the NBA rakes in about $10 billion in annual revenue as of 2023, the WNBA generates $60 million; the highest paid NBA player earns $48 million while the highest paid WNBA player can only hope to make $228,094 a year (Janvrin, 2023). The disparity here is astounding, and this only covers one professionally-played sport. In short, the work performed by females is undervalued: Women who work full-time are only paid an average of 83.7% of what their male counterparts receive for the same work (Chun-Hoon, 2023). This means that for every dollar a man makes, your daughter will only earn 83 cents. She'll be running her entire life trying to catch up, financially-speaking.

A substantial portion of helping your daughter see her value will be up to you to instill a healthy degree of her self-worth, well before she becomes old enough to worry about employment. There will also be television programs, music, ads, photoshopped images, peer pressure, and social media that present her with the false idea that if she is "perfect" or up to a certain beauty standard, she will be rewarded well in life. And if she is anything less, she is (worth)less.

By the time your daughter reaches age 13, she will have viewed over 520,000 advertisements on TV alone that have influenced her development and sense of self-worth in some way—millions more via other avenues like on social media apps and in magazine pages (Dittmann, 2004). That's a lot of potentially negative influence that directly combats whatever body-positive encouragement she receives at home. This is your mantle to carry on and instill in her: That your daughter is beautiful, smart, capable, and amazing regardless of any flaws she may see in herself. She is everything good in this world and adds so much more to your world than just her good looks that make her a prize to look at or how politely demure she is to others so they feel good about themselves. She is your little girl, and her life holds more value than mere beauty and people-pleasing.

Give her ample opportunities to be more. Let her help you when you're working around the house. Explain how tools work, what is their use, what are their names, and how to hold them properly. Likewise, you should sit with her and let her explain to you how something she enjoys works. Ask her open-ended questions like, "Why did you choose this makeup brush over this one?" and "Is there a reason behind your liking this artist's music instead of this artist?"

The goal is to get to know your daughter at her level of development. The topic of conversation will change as she grows and her interests change, but the goal remains the same: Take every opportunity to invest in your child before they are taxed with facing the cruelties of the world on their own. As you ask your daughter about her interests, she will open up to you about other topics, too. This process builds trust that you are listening. You are interested in her world.

She interprets this attention as, "I am interesting and worth getting to know." And when the pressures present in life become too much for her to carry alone, she will be more likely to turn to you to help her gain direction, perspective, or just have someone to listen to without expectation or wanting something in return.

You are her sounding board, her audience, and her place of refuge from all the negative things she will face in life. It's not going to be an easy job to sit, listen, and keep opinions to yourself. You'll need to filter through those internally, choosing your words carefully, before you speak. But keeping her heart intact is worth the extra effort because the open world won't afford her the same buffered experience.

The most important thing you can do as her father is to always be the safety she can return home to instead of the storm she needs to avoid her whole life. As the historically-held role of head-of-household, you hold the majority of the power, control, and direction over what goes on, is allowed, is scheduled, and is acceptable in your home. It's the general default 'way of the world' that has been standard practice throughout the world for ages.

There are exceptions to every rule; there are a few societies that practice matriarchy where women rule the roost. The Khasi tribe of India own and pass down property, land, wealth, and other possessions only through their maternal bloodline. The family surname is also taken from the maternal side (is matrilineal) rather than everyone taking the father's last name as their own, as is customary in most Western cultures (as in a patriarchy).

Whatever the power dynamics are in your home, you should attempt to maintain an equal hand in household chores, bringing in income, making and enforcing rules, setting boundaries, being respectful, and prioritizing and anticipating everyone's needs. Strive to impart to each family member how they are supposed to pull their own weight, equally, working together toward the same goal: a household that runs smoothly and has everything they need to perform their best.

When you dictate orders to be completed to others and then sit out, not contributing the same effort or reducing yourself to perform the same tasks, you're conveying a message that you're superior. You remove yourself from being on an equal level as everyone else in your household. To yell, scream, berate, curse, and stomp around during an argument creates a further divide.

Your children will fear you. Your partner will feel like they are left to pick up all the pieces. Everyone will walk by you on tiptoes afraid to trigger a fresh round of tyranny. Having someone respect you is not the same as having someone fear you. The reason for keeping in line just so your father won't rip your head off is vastly different from doing the right thing for the right reasons. You want your daughter to find motivation in making you proud of her, delighting in her accomplishments, and not have her compete to please or appease you so you won't hurt her.

If you have trouble controlling your anger at home but find yourself keeping it all bottled up at work, you know that it's a matter of intent rather than being out of control. No one can control all the events or outcomes of any given situation. Life is unpredictable like that. But what you can control is how you react. You can choose the words you use and the actions you perform. You can keep yourself from throwing objects, raising your voice, and storming out when you're angry.

Tell your family you're upset and need a moment to cool off. Go for a walk, workout; do something physical like scrubbing the bathroom clean. Remove yourself from letting the issue escalate beyond anything you imagined. Permanent damage to your children's psyche, their relationship with you, their view of you, and your relationship with your partner can happen more quickly than it can be solved or repaired.

The way you prevent causing harm, making your children fear you, and responsibly handle challenging situations is to remain calm even if you want to scream and tear through all the walls in your house. Rage is a continual building of "big feelings" (as we tell our little ones). When you don't release these emotions like anger, disappointment, embarrassment, frustration, and fear, they stack one on top of another until you feel like you can't take it anymore. You might lash out, say things you don't truly mean, and you'll end up beginning the process of severing your relationships with people you love.

Try to take those feelings and focus all that energy into something mindless (like playing a video game, playing catch, undertaking yard work, or working on automotives) and something that requires physical exertion.

If you blow up more than once, it becomes a habit, and this extremely detrimental behavior is harder to break. It transforms into part of the legacy you leave behind for your children. Even if you apologize, it just becomes empty words once you continually do the same behavior over and over that you claimed you were "sorry" for having committed. Saying "sorry" only works when it's paired with changed behavior.

You may cause your daughter to become desensitized to this kind of verbal and emotional abuse. This would, in turn, leave her susceptible to also becoming the victim of physical and sexual abuse if she thinks of any form of abuse as a "normal" way for someone to behave. Don't set the dangerous precedent that any amount or form of abuse is acceptable. It is not.

More than that, your daughter may find herself adopting any controlling behaviors she witnesses you enact. She may also desperately spend her life trying to maintain control over even the tiniest pieces of her life because she spent her childhood in a constant state of turmoil and chaos at your hand, your temper.

Girls who are raised by aggressive fathers have a harder time accepting themselves and they are more vulnerable to having body image issues, eating disorders, act more fearful or timid, and have less confidence because they've internalized a fear of authority. Any action or image of herself she fears will set off a volatile father can cause your daughter to strive to be "perfect" and deride herself when she falls short.

No one is ever going to get it right every single time, but you can guide your daughter away from the hazards of internalizing your bad behaviors. Take her hands and apologize earnestly whenever you lose your cool or say something you wish you could take back. She will still remember what you said and visualize how you behaved, but she will also remember that you apologized immediately, and that you were truly sorry for having hurt her.

Being a dad and being a man isn't something shameful or villainous. You are the only person who can fulfill your role as dad. But, you should know that your actions and words have a greater impact on how your daughter interprets the social, cultural, and physical expectations placed upon her. She will label her worth wherever you set the bar. So if you allow yourself to hurt her in any way, she will remain locked at that level. It will be incredibly difficult for her to believe she doesn't have to demean herself just because that's always how it's been done and she never had anyone tell her or treat her like it could be any different.

Don't fade into the shadows like the other monsters that will haunt her as she takes on the world. She'll meet plenty of other villains who want to tear her down when she's on her own. Your job is to make her feel invincible because she is the most beautiful soul you'll ever know. Build worlds for her to conquer instead of letting venom slip out during a heated moment that will eat away her confidence. You want her to hear echoes of your praise and love instead of placing every other person she meets into your shoes to see if they make her feel as small as you used to.

You can be her hero no matter how young or old either of you are. It's never too late to build or rebuild your daughter back to where you know she belongs.

There may be vices and villains in her life that she battles every single day (some are substantial and others are small, but they add up). Even as a child, there are microaggressions that tear her from her ability to smile, laugh, and enjoy life to its fullest. Look at your daughter often. Notice her eyes, her posture, and what she chooses to do when she has down-time. Does she look tired and her shoulders slump? Does she have less energy? Does she want to sleep when she used to enjoy singing or dancing with you during silly moments?

Telltale signs that your daughter is happy is if she feels "light" enough to want to sing, dance, or be creative. These are artistic avenues that well-nourished souls express their emotions through when all their other, most basic, needs are being met.

If you notice changes in your daughter's normal behavior, it's time to sit down at a quiet moment with your daughter and check-in to see if she's okay. Chances are that this will only be a starter conversation and she might not feel ready to discuss anything that's bothering her yet. Be willing to drop everything at a moment's notice when she *is* ready to talk to you.

Begin with a non-aggressive opener like, "It looks like you haven't been as energetic or haven't been singing as much or have been sleeping a lot more during the day than you used to. If something is troubling you, you can always tell me. I'm ready to listen to whatever you want to share with me. No judgment. I won't be upset no matter what it is."

You can follow this with a solid, "I'm always here for you, any time of day or night." Your daughter might need additional time to prepare or sort out her thoughts before she's ready to divulge everything substantial, but at least you've opened the door so that she can access you. If she does tell you what's troubling her, then you can always ask her, "Is there anything I can do to help?"

This question holds immense value because it doesn't assume she needs help, but it does provide the possibility that you are there if and when she thinks she's ready to accept your help. It will get her to think about how you could help. It shows her that she is not alone in handling anything life throws at her.

Your daughter will learn how to ask for help and that it isn't shameful to do so. Humans aren't meant to live in solitude, handling all of life's hardships alone. When she can count on you to be the same person with the same reaction—neutral without condemnation—your daughter will view you as a safe person who has her best interests at heart. She will grow to rely on you. This trust is paramount to her ability to identify similar characteristics in potential suitors. If she sees warning signs, she will know that she deserves better.

The Importance of Communication and Open Dialogue

The main way you will foster a strong bond with your daughter is by looking at her as she speaks, and practicing active listening by nodding your head every once in a while and offering a quiet "yeah" or "uh huh" to let her know you're listening. Save the advice or judgment for the big battles like if she uses substances that would cause her harm. Being able to listen is equally as important as concisely expressing your needs to someone else. Perhaps, listening is the more difficult of the two to accomplish, but it is the most valuable tool in your fatherhood tool kit.

You will listen to how she arranges the rules of her games as you play with her toys with her or play a board game and provide the appropriate support to the role she has assigned you. She will also learn your rules as you teach her how sports like baseball and soccer work. Just as she needs to understand that her boundaries are important and to be respected, she equally needs to know that the world has rules that must be followed, too.

When you communicate effectively (this means that the message being conveyed is both given and received in its intended form) then you will notice an increase in how easy it feels to talk to your child, and how natural it is for them to respond to you or even to strike up a conversation with you on their own. This happens, of course, once your child acquires the skill of speech necessary to facilitate language mastery.

Your first line of communication with your newborn occurs well before she is born. Most fetuses acquire functioning audiological and the necessary neurological processing systems as early as 12-18 weeks gestation when the small hairlike structures develop inside the fetal ear canal in the cochlea. All of these features convert vibrations outside the ear canal to be interpreted by the brain, internally; the first sounds that a fetus hears occur inside the mother's body, like her heartbeat (Boyd-Barrett, 2021). The outside ear structure develops first, followed by the special mechanisms inside the cochlea that detect sound frequencies, and then specialized neurotransmitters begin functioning to act as a pathway between the microscopic hair cells and the brain that will transform that signal into sound perception the infant understands.

In essence your daughter will be able to discern your voice from her mother's voice at around the six to seven month mark in the pregnancy (Shu, 2021). You may find that your infant will turn her head as she tries to "track" where your voice is coming from if you're moving around the room once she's born because your voice is a familiar sound she likes.

Even when she cannot verbalize a response, your attentive and calming effect as her father whenever she cries and you respond will be her first lesson in how to trust someone else. Try not to let her "cry it out" as popular sleep-training methods will instruct you. Infants are only able to communicate in one way when they are born—that is to cry whenever they are hungry, hurt, over-tired, or generally in need of help.

Babies aren't able to self-soothe unless they are taught how to cope with their overwhelming sense of urgency at having an empty tummy. Inside the womb, babies never experience the sensation of having hunger pangs because they constantly ingest and urinate amniotic fluid so their digestive tract is always "full." This new feeling of hunger can be alarming to a newborn who needs to learn and process these new sensations, what they mean, and how to correct them so that all their needs are met.

When you respond immediately to her cries, your daughter begins to learn that you will be there to take care of her. The more gentle and attentive you are from the beginning, the easier it will be to deepen the relationship to one where she feels she can confide the more complicated or embarrassing parts of her life with you.

Strategies for Building a Strong, Positive Relationship

In preparation for lifting 200 pounds, you would begin by repeatedly lifting weights of a lower heaviness. The same can be said of how you would go about building a strong foundation with your daughter during the "easier" years when she is more child than teen because the heavy stuff is sometimes too grueling for her to carry alone. The weight becomes more cumbersome with age.

Mature problems require additional support and your daughter will turn to you as her chosen person if you have shown you are trustworthy, non-judgemental, calm, and present up to that point. Sure, you'll have lost your cool a time or two—you're only human; we all make mistakes. Sincere apologies go a long way to repairing any trust lost in the fray.

Seek outside help for yourself if you need to work beyond what you know how to navigate on your own. No one person is born knowing the best way or where to look for help. If you are not the most nurturing version of yourself because daily stressors have infiltrated and eroded away your ability to function without lashing out, your family will suffer. It takes more courage to ask for help than to suffer in silence when you don't have to. There is no weakness in admitting when you are overwhelmed.

Discuss what happens before you erupt in a rage and how you could have prevented losing your temper. Oftentimes, just talking to a professional helps elucidate the circumstances more clearly so that you can identify the problem areas you can change for the better. Your daughter will see you putting in the work, she will see that seeking help isn't a weakness. Knowing yourself is an unmatched strength.

Your daughter will learn to trust herself, she will see you as a trustworthy person, too. Only you can stop the generational trauma you've endured in the past from damaging your daughter now, and perpetrating more harm from which the next generation will cower away. Abuse can stop with you so that she doesn't end up feeling like you did when no one stepped in to protect you from undue rage or shame directed at you.

The effort you put in now will culminate in a level of trust your daughter will be more likely to exercise when she needs help. Friends, schoolwork, extracurricular activities, relationships that might blossom into more, and personal interests are all part of learning who your child is and how they might need you to fit into their world. Get to know her in all of these major areas that affect her so as to open up a constant line of two-way access for each of you to comfortably approach one another about any topic either of you needs to discuss. Learn your daughter's style of communication and pay close attention to beauty images, fashion trends, and diet fads that seem to be popular. Those things can also affect your daughter in ways you hadn't thought of before.

If your daughter has extra skin that sticks out in certain outfits, try to be encouraging especially when she tells you that the outfit feels comfortable. If the weather is sunny and hot, expect that she will probably wear something that shows more skin because she shouldn't suffocate under layers of clothing in the name of "modesty" when her male peers are permitted to go shirtless.

If your daughter's wearing spaghetti straps and shorts, let her be comfortable and enjoy her summer without saying things that make her feel ashamed for having been born a girl. The purpose of clothes isn't to hide parts of our figures that are unflattering or to attempt to control the lustful thoughts of the opposite sex. Attire is used to express our individuality so that we are comfortable in our fabric "skin" as we take on the world and simply exist.

Try your hardest to stay neutral, nonjudgmental and encouraging when communicating with your daughter. If she repeatedly gets flack for telling you the things she's interested in, criticized for what she's wearing or how she feels, and is minimized in her opinions then she will turn to you less and less. Don't be a pushover by any means, but realize that the things she says and whatever she chooses to do in life is important to her.

Your daughter is not a carbon copy of you or your partner. She's an individual that you are blessed with 17 summers to watch her grow into the independent, capable woman she will become when she is ready to spread her wings to depart the nest you've built for her to thrive in. She's worth every amount of effort to maintain that relationship and level of trust. If she chooses to come back home to visit or stay a little longer, you'll know you've done everything in your power to create a comfortable, safe place for her with you.

Chapter 2
The Role of Fathers in Their Daughter's Development

Now that you know what your role in your daughter's life is supposed to be, we'll begin to explore your unique role in your child's development. Your presence is of an unparalleled importance to your daughter's social, physical, mental, academic, and social development.

The bond she forms with you early on will determine her ability to achieve success in all areas of her adult life. How she views herself, what she will and won't accept from a future partner, and what she believes she is capable of handling and achieving ultimately rests in your ability to convey to her time and again that she already is all these things, is deserving of, and is capable of making her own dreams become a reality.

Your role is to lift her up, to be ready to catch her should she fall. Let her down easy when disappointment is inevitable. As her father, you are the first person who holds her heart; breaking it, belittling, pushing her aside in favor of something else, and pointing out any of her flaws will undermine the solid relationship you are trying to nurture.

Just like you have changed her diapers, cleaned her cuts when-ever she falls, and held her hand to help steady her as she learns to walk, you should make yourself available to her whenever she seeks your advice. Rush to her when she scrapes her knee. But to build a more resilient spirit, it's best to not "baby" her when she's hurt. "I know it hurts" and "Try to breathe while we clean the wound," will set a more realistic expectation for what pain is and how to handle it (like rubbing a sore spot such as an elbow or knee that she bumped to lessen the painful sensation).

Help her with her homework when she seems stumped. Offer an encouraging, "Do you *want* help with that?" instead of using an assuming phrase like, "Do you *need* help?" There is a difference in tone and implication between the words "want" and "need" that imply it is her choice to accept assistance instead of you assuming she cannot complete the task on her own. Never step in if it takes her longer to figure out a viable solution. This, too, can imply that she's taking too long and should just hurry up. She'll doubt herself and her ability to finish a task.

This and exaggerating everyday bumps and bruises will create a damsel: Someone who seeks the attention she receives when she needs rescuing. Let the princess save herself.

It might seem silly—a small choice of words shouldn't have the ability to tear down someone's confidence... But it does. Word choices matter. They will echo in your child's mind for decades. Make the most of this time in her formative years or salvage all you can of the relationship with your older daughter.

We are not guaranteed an infinite number of days, but we have the opportunity to put in the effort needed now if we are to make lasting bonds with our children before they are grown.

Even if your daughter is an adult, your presence in her life is still valuable and can be made anew if you are patient with your unassuming effort to listen to her and how she feels, what she thinks, and what role she needs you to occupy in her life. It is never too late to listen to your child.

A Unique Role

When an active father is present in his daughter's everyday doings, she is capable of accomplishing the impossible.

Dr. Margaret J. Meeker researched and wrote a book on this very topic where she discovered that "a daughter's self-esteem is best predicted by her father's loving affection" (Plowman, 2018). As an accomplished pediatrician, Meeker made connections between a daughter's toddlerhood and how facets of her entire life would be impacted by the stability of this one relationship.

There is no replacement for your position as your daughter's father. Only you can fulfill that role. Your daughter will become what you make of it or choose to neglect. She will forever seek your approval, admiration, respect, affection, and attention. Her life is ultimately what you make of it as you choose how you respond to her cries for her needs being met.

From the moment she is born, your baby cries whenever she needs affection, to be fed, or changed, or simply to be held. She is able to hear your voice as early as six months gestation, inside her mother's womb. When she is born, she will discern your voice from a room full of voices as one she recognizes. She will turn her head to "track" you when she hears you speak.

From the moment she is able to hear you, your daughter will learn to look for you—as rescue, as support, and as anything and everything she or you could never fathom until the need arises. You are her world. She will learn everything by watching you, listening to you, and observing whatever you choose to do or not do.

This level of importance in any person's life can be quite heady, but so is the level of responsibility for how well or how poorly attached your child will be in forming her own relationships as she becomes a young adult. Her relationship with her mother will be completely different from your role. Make no mistake that yours is vital and equal to that of her mother's, but it is different and supports a different function of reassurance, support, skills, and protection from the real monsters present in the real world.

Only you can be her father; read on to learn how to make the most of that vital role.

How to Be a Positive Role Model

With too many obligations pulling at you from all angles, it can feel overwhelming when you get home from work to have a tiny creature pawing at you for affection and attention. But your daughter's self-worth is on the line at all times. She craves your attention, she wants you to see her.

Take a few moments when you get home for yourself by gently explaining (if you are met with a huge hug or a grappling of gangly limbs) to your child that Daddy needs a few moments to get himself together after a long day and then he is ready for full-attention daddy time—her choice of activity. A side note here, if your partner works (as a stay-at-home parent or outside the home), they may also need a few moments, or a grace period, to collect themselves so that they can be the best version of themselves during the transition to family time.

Being respectful of your partner and their time will help you model a healthy relationship for your child to emulate.

Other ways to help solidify your relationship is to talk to your daughter on her level, crouch down to eye-level, using words tailored to her level of understanding whatever age she is. Keep your cool even when you're angry at times. Emotions are okay to display; they are appropriate reactions to stressful situations. But they need to be expressed in a healthy way for all parties involved.

If you yell, curse, or lose your cool at any point, the best thing you can do is use it as a teaching moment for your child (especially if they witnessed the blow up). Calmly sit with your child to have a heart-to-heart about how even adults let their emotions get the better of them sometimes.

While it's okay to be angry, it's not okay to belittle or scare someone. Apologies and acknowledging the hurt you caused goes a long way to showing the child that people make mistakes. No one is perfect. It is *how* we handle conflict and confrontations that determines how strong or how broken our relationships will be.

Mend broken trust by stating you were wrong, you will make a conscious effort to do better, and you expect others to behave the same. Model the expectation you have for your child. Everything can become a teaching moment if you take the time to frame it as such while sitting calmly with your child so that they have your full attention.

Explain that better ways to handle such big emotions is to walk away, take a walk, write about it, do something that demands physical activity so that all those negative emotions (like sadness and anger) have a healthy outlet or release from your body instead of directing it at someone else in a dangerous or unhealthy manner. Take deep breaths and think before you speak.

Words can be the most powerful tool humans use, a father's words hold more power than most. Just as you may remember the painful words used or ways your parents or other adults treated you as a child, your child, too, will remember the lasting effects of what you say, and even what you remain silent about for years to come.

Treat strangers as you would someone you were trying to impress. They are humans, too, with feelings, dreams, and a purpose. You want your little one to see the humanity and importance of every soul they encounter because they are the future charged with the impossibly monumental task of leading the next generation. If your daughter sees you taking the time to help someone else, no matter what their station in life is, with no reward in it for you, she will understand that she is the kindness that will change the world for the better. She will be more likely to stand up for what she believes and for those who cannot speak up for themselves. Her confidence will grow because she will see her world change because of your positive influence and actions.

Stay mindful of your words, actions, and inaction because your daughter is always watching. The best way to be a positive role model is to *be* the hero she already knows you are by filtering every interaction through the eyes of your child and how she would react if she were to witness what you've done. Don't let her down if you can help it. We're all human and prone to fail at some point. Own your mistakes, take responsibility, and apologize as needed. No matter how old she grows, your daughter is always that little girl who looks to you when things break, to be her superglue holding her together.

Strategies for Instilling Confidence and Self-Worth

Every day is an opportunity to teach your daughter to trust in herself, her confidence, and grow her self-worth. With this philosophy, it follows that there are a multitude of infinite moments throughout each and everyday that you can reinforce positivity for your child. Seize every chance, no matter how small, to lift your daughter up—literally and metaphorically.

When she is small and you are younger, take every opportunity to hold your daughter. Cuddle her close to teach her she is safe in your arms. As she grows more steady to navigate her environment on her own, stay close by in case she stumbles or looks over her shoulder to make sure you're watching her as she begins to take on the world. Your attention and approval is not overtly expressed as needed, but is nevertheless desperately needed during these instances of "Look what I can do, Dad!" and "Look at what I made, isn't it pretty?"

Always be encouraging. Tell your daughter that she's funny, unique, special, and truly there is no one else on the entire planet who could ever compare to her and how much you love her. The more you believe in her, the more she will believe in herself.

Tell her every chance you can find just how wonderful she is; drop everything to shower her with praise, attention, and hold her until she's too grown for that. Then, hug her.

The best thing about instilling confidence in someone else is that it's never too late to build someone else up. It may only take a short instance of mispeaking or lashing out to crush confidence, but it can be rebuilt (like trust). With effort and determination mixed with sincerity, you can always remake that bridge to your little girl no matter how old she is. Keep showing up when she needs you or asks you to be around.

Remember: You are her father. No one else can build up your daughter like you can.

When You've Tried Everything and Nothing Seems to Be Working

A failsafe for resetting your child's mood when they are having trouble regulating their behavior themselves is to (gently and metaphorically) toss them into the tub for a bath. Let them soak in the tepid water for a while before beginning to clean them, or letting them scrub themselves if they're at that level of independence.

Enlist the help of bath toys, pouring cups, water wheels, or other tangible ways they can manipulate the water as the stress they felt previously begins to release itself into their new, aquatic environment.

As discussed earlier, a child is unable to reset themselves without guidance. Children don't come pre-programmed on how to regulate their emotional responses. As her parent, you will often need to instigate a kind of manual "reset" for her by removing the trigger from her sight, or by physically taking the child into a different room so that she can begin to calm down. With the external stimuli gone, no longer able to keep causing stimulation, your child's body begins to return to its typical homeostasis (level zero) where your child can focus and is able to listen to the lesson on why she shouldn't have been doing what she had been.

Overstimulated individuals of any age are unable to be receptive, focus, listen, or learn anything new until they calm down because their body and brain are instead in a heightened state of fight or flight, a panic response to danger. You know that there is no danger present, but a small child's body or someone who has never learned how to control their emotions, only feels their blood pressure, pulse, and breathing increase rapidly.

If you aren't somewhere where you can let your daughter cool off in the bathtub, try breathing with her. Breathe in deeply and slowly as you hug your child so that she feels how calm you are. Her body processes will slow to match yours in a matter of minutes. Holding your child will also prevent her from accidentally hurting herself if she's in full tantrum mode. Just be sure to avert your face, nose, and other more sensitive areas of your body as you do so. Think offensively how to avoid being headbutted or losing a tooth.

When your daughter seems more alert, more herself, sit with her on your lap or just beside you. Ask, "How do you feel about how you behaved?" She will probably tell you that she knows what she did is wrong and that she's sorry. If she doesn't, you will need to calmly explain that what she did was dangerous or could have resulted in "XYZ". It's okay to say that you love her but that you still expect more from her, to listen instead of losing control.

You have a reason for every rule you've laid out, it isn't to make her life boring or more difficult. Even if she doesn't understand the reasons why right now, one day soon she will.

When you are in control of your emotions during such a highly volatile tantrum, you will help your daughter's confidence improve. It may sound ridiculous. But if she is literally unable to control herself, she needs to be able to count on you to help her through such a potentially scary time when she cannot verbalize what's wrong or why she's upset.

In time, your daughter will learn the names of her emotions. With your help, she will also learn how to cope with disappointment, loss, embarrassment, heartache, anger, and fear. You may also need to help her calm down in times when she is overexcited for good reasons like she's at her favorite musicians' most epic concert and she just can't calm down. Keep an eye on her in case she faints in times like this. There is little else you can do.

By being vigilant, noticing the most minute changes in your daughter's demeanor, you will be able to tell when something is "off" and she needs your assistance. By being there often, you will know her nuances, her mannerisms, her inside jokes, and her personal details. She'd rather die than let anyone else in the whole world know certain details of her life, with you as the exception.

Earning her trust by being the "bad guy" in high-conflict situations like tantrums means that she can anticipate your support in other, more complicated matters when she's older. You had confidence in her abilities first, so she will know that she can master her emotions because you first showed her how it is done.

Dress for Success, and for Fun!

Letting your daughter choose the outfits she wants to wear not only builds her self-esteem, but it also allows for greater creative expression. She needs to be comfortable in excessively hot weather, and for all seasons. She should also be comfortable in her own skin without having to worry about what the boy behind her in class thinks about her bare shoulders or thighs showing when she's in a skirt.

When you are worried about someone taking advantage of your little girl, which is a realistic fear, you can have her wear short shorts underneath her skirt so that when she plays "like a boy" on the playground or turns a cartwheel, her underwear doesn't show. This option gives her the freedom to play however makes her heart content without being told constantly to put her legs together or to keep her skirt down.

This illustrates a significant difference in how boys are raised versus how girls are raised. "Boys will be boys" and girls will be held to unattainable standards to compensate. This is how the world works in too many societies. Excuses and exclusions are made for certain individuals but not everyone receives the same punishments.

When societal and economic systems are put in place that prevent your daughter from easily leaving an abusive partner or reporting an atrocity, we can safely say that not all individuals are treated equally no matter what our personal experience is with cause and effect. Most judges side biasly in divorce matters. Regardless of how poorly her domestic partner treated your daughter during their relationship, he will still be granted access to her to further perpetuate any abuse he desires if they share children.

It can break down her confidence at every turn when she feels like she keeps hitting her head up against a wall when trying to flee or be completely free from someone who destroys everything good in her life. All that you worked to build up in her becomes fractured into tinier and tinier fragments of her former self.

You see all your hard work, all you've seen your daughter accomplish, disappear beneath bruises and sunken shoulders. Rightly so, you may feel your rage ignite like a furnace ready to leave the entire city where the abuser resides in smoldering ashes. But you are just as powerless to stop his advances as your daughter.

She's up against legal systems, laws, professionals, and prejudiced people who won't be swayed even when the facts are indisputable. Liars, lawyers, and villains tend to stick up for one another. The only way you will be able to help your daughter get out of her abusive relationship is to let her take refuge with you in your home if you can. Listen to her. Believe her at all costs even when the person she's been with has seemed nothing short of sweet every time you met them. Monsters tend to hide behind closed doors.

That's how prevalent and inconspicuous abuse is. It happens everywhere, in more subtle ways than in noticeable ways. But it kills you slowly all the same.

The exception is when the victim tries to leave. They tell themselves in the beginning that it was only once. It was an accident or a mistake. They try to convince themselves that it won't happen again. But when it does, they create new excuses for that behavior, too. And so it goes in a cycle of raw emotion and hurt after the incident, then the honeymoon period of "I'm sorry's" and promises that they will change. They won't make the same mistakes again.

Until they succeed. And it escalates to the point that the victim would rather leave all of their worldly possessions behind just to make the pain stop, to survive. To get away, they would risk it all. And when the victim leaves, the abuser pursues—sometimes in the most dangerous ways. Each victim of domestic abuse risks a 75% chance of being murdered when they try to leave the relationship (*Definition of domestic violence*, 2019). That percentage is true in every attempt they make to end the relationship.

Not every person who is abused is able to leave the first time they try. Fear of the unknown, fear of retaliation (of getting it worse than ever before), and fear of being unable to care for themselves and their children often bring a victim right back to the abuser in time, unless she has a solid support system to help her at every turn.

Teach your daughter how to spot red flags or warning signs in relationships early on as you watch shows on TV, the news, and real-life relationships of people she knows so that she can identify these abusive behaviors in others when the time comes.

Controlling someone else's future is a huge red flag. Making unnecessary comments that leave your daughter feeling degraded or small is another. If the other person only makes choices based on their position in the relationship without considering how it will affect their partner, this, too, is another warning sign that perhaps this person isn't in it for a recipro-cal, egalitarian relationship that is mutually beneficial or aligned to both parties' interests for the future.

The optimal way to prevent her from falling for any line these predators throw out as bait is to tell your daughter how amazing she is, how important she is to you, and how much you hope she finds someone one day who will consider her heart and happiness first. You want her to find someone who will keep her safe and whole at all times. If the person of her interests consistently builds her up or breaks her down, you will know.

You've hopefully laid all the groundwork for your daughter long before any person of interest enters the picture, just how cherished she is. She will probably search for a person who behaves, looks, or has interests similar to yours. Make sure you're modeling healthy behaviors for her to emulate and admire. Give her the tools she needs to problem-solve on her own. It's not as difficult as it sounds to do these things. It takes effort, knowing when to step back and watch your little girl give it a try on her own, and patience.

Sometimes, your daughter will fail. You will make mistakes, too. Momentary failure is a teaching moment. Each broken bone, bruised ego, and wrong turn teaches us what to do differently next time to avoid defeat. You might be thinking that you're saving your daughter from getting hurt by catching her fall or preventing her from taking the plunge in the first place. But this is untrue. Being so tight-fisted when it comes to "allowing" your daughter to engage her free will only make her feel repressed.

Repression is dangerous in that it leaves her feeling like a failure without having ever attempted the very thing she "failed" at in her mind. She will be left to wonder, "What if?" And one day, when you aren't there to hold her back, she will act on those thoughts. She won't have you there to teach her how to control the outcome or to pick up the very real pieces of what she's done without you as her safety net.

Children find a way to sneak around, often making impulsive and detrimental choices. They will find a way even when you've told them time and again that this is going to hurt them. They could develop an addiction. They could end up pregnant or the school joke. You know because you have experienced the contextual consequences of making mistakes that altered the course of your own life. Life experience is funny like that. When you have nothing to compare, no prior knowledge, you don't know what to expect and so you make a blind leap into whatever fallout happens afterward.

Hindsight affords individuals all the knowledge they wish they knew before they made such a life-altering choice. So even if you've expended all your energy trying to warn and explain any coming catastrophe, your daughter is ultimately going to make up her own mind. She will face the consequences (yours for broken rules or natural ones that are beyond your control) on her own. You've done all you can to prepare your little girl to take her place and make her way, but at least she can still look to you if she fails at her endeavors working out as she had planned. It's all about how you welcome her back home that will keep her confident that she is still loved even when she messes up.

Chapter 3
Nurturing Your Daughter's Talents and Passions

To piggyback off the last chapter, you will notice that as your daughter develops, she will take on varied interests that all work to help her build confidence as she discovers who she is and what she likes. These activities might include gymnastics, singing, various types of dance, baseball, soccer, and other social sports, athletic, and artistic avenues for her creative expression. All you need to do is listen to her incredibly valid excitement over anything she dreams to pursue, foot the bill, provide the supplies, and cheer from the balcony, bleachers, sidelines, and crowd.

Be the loudest dad in the group: Just go for it—have no shame! Your daughter might say she's "embarrassed," but she will never doubt your commitment to helping her succeed or that you are beaming with pride at all she is capable of doing.

Strategies for Discovering and Supporting Your Daughter's Interests and Talents

Even the smallest achievements aren't perceived as "small" to your child. The art she creates, the grades she earns, and the practice on her fourth grade recorder all mean something *more* to your daughter. It's all a testament to her hard work and she wants you to validate, to see, and recognize her as "good" and "worthy" of your praise.

It may sound childish, but that's because it kind of is. You're teaching your child how to perform positive "self-talk" where their inner voice will sound like you are speaking praise, or criticism, for the rest of their life. Your child will remember exactly how you react, what you say, and how you say it during times when they seek your approval most.

This can be when they get home from school or when you get home from work and your daughter is eager to share something exciting with you. Try your hardest to recognize the higher inflection in your child's voice, the way they bounce to greet you, so that you understand this is an important moment in your child's life. Be present for it.

Ways to test what might spark your child's interests include exposing her to different approaches to create art (paint, markers, crayons, and digitally), read to her every day, and sing to your child. Even if your voice isn't the greatest, your daughter doesn't care. So croon out the silliest songs because the melody lights up the parts of her brain responsible for analytics and mathematics. She'll need this stimulation when she enters school and also to help develop critical thinking.

It's not coddling or disingenuous to build your child up for the amount of work they put into their achievements. One thing to avoid when offering praise is to praise the child as being merely "beautiful," "smart," or "good" because these are fleeting physical attributes or place the emphasis on results instead of on the amazing child and her hard work ethic. These are essential (even though your daughter may be too young to understand their importance right now) to build up her self-confidence and ability to believe in herself without relying on others to tell her she's pretty or this or that thing that makes her valuable. Try to explain in more words exactly what your daughter did right so that she can replicate the action that generated praise.

Children are observant: They hear everything we wish they wouldn't and see exactly how we say one thing and do another. So be sure to listen to your little girl and give her the reins to help her chase her dreams. Let her take up any sport or hobby within your budget. And show enthusiasm for the hard work she puts in so that it pays off for both of you to bring you closer together as she simultaneously gains independence.

The Importance of Letting Your Daughter Stretch Her Wings

The importance of getting your daughter to experience a variety of different creative outlets and opportunities cannot be stressed enough. She needs to know what's out there, available and within her reach, or she may struggle to find her passion, talent, and purpose for her own life as she ages. It's never too soon to begin fostering your daughter's creativity.

Begin as early as birth by offering her different textured toys with vibrant colors, pastels, and monochrome tones on different days. Do the same for soft versus hard or bumpy objects. She's never felt the softness of a down blanket or the crinkly texture of a baby book made for these stimuli exercises.

The thought behind this is to highlight or activate the separate parts of her brain that perceive differences in texture, tone, vibrancy, and other characteristics that acclimate her to the world around her without overwhelming her senses. When a child's environment is too loud, busy, or distracting, they will have a harder time focusing on what you're trying to teach them. So be sure to limit the background noise and sights as much as possible during these teaching moments.

When your baby and you are ready, begin taking her out into the world through outings and exploring her own neighborhood while on a walk. You can safely start taking your baby out in public around large crowds once their immune system is more hardy. This will be around six months of age (once they've gotten their first round of childhood vaccinations). Before that, you may choose to limit your child's exposure to other people who don't share a household with your child because some germs, viruses, bacteria, fungi, and other pathogens can cause devastating illnesses and have lifelong consequences that may impede her development.

When you let your little girl explore her world by crawling, then walking, then running, and eventually swimming and climbing, she will realize that the future is full of wondrous surprises just waiting for her to discover them. It's imperative that you are as much a part of that developing curiosity as you can be because she will require your help in bandaging the bruises and repairing her broken heart when the best-laid plans go awry.

While you cannot prevent every injury, you can weigh the benefit of letting your child discover her world unencumbered by parental judgment and preventing the more dangerous or criminal behaviors young adults tend to make.

Like a toddler throwing a tantrum, repeating the same behavior you told them to stop a few moments ago, teenagers will test the boundaries of their environment. This means also testing the limitations of your love and willingness to let boundary crossings slide.

The best course of action to engage when your daughter knowingly crosses the boundary you've put in place is to remain firm and consistent. Consistency is key! When you react with the same punishment (grounding, taking away loved items, and restricting access to rewards) every time a rule is broken, your daughter will anticipate your reaction. She should adjust her behavior to meet your expectations.

It will be frustrating. You may feel like you're talking to a wall, but your tactics are working even if she continues to betray your trust. Stay focused as you stick to the consequence you've warned would occur if your rule were broken. Nothing you do in the realm of parenthood should surprise your child so keep your expectations the same from age zero to age 18.

Your daughter will begin to expect the same reaction from you if she performs a certain action. Whether your daughter is a baby and she learns that hitting hurts because you put her gently back on the ground after she hurts you while you were holding her. Or if you ground her from using her bike if she stays out past when the streetlights come on. Or, even if she's older and takes the car for a spin without asking first, your daughter should know when she's crossed the line of acceptable behavior and to expect a consequence equal to the infraction.

Pick your battles. You will always be her hero, but that doesn't mean you have to act like you're her "friend." You're her father and your priority is to keep her safe at all times. If you know that her actions are going to lead her somewhere unsafe or unhealthy, by all means, help your daughter understand that she's going to get hurt and you love her more than letting her disappointment dictate you letting her walk into a situation that will cause her pain.

Watch from afar as she embarks on her many journeys into becoming the person she will be as an adult. Guide her with wisdom, tell her stories that will teach her, and always tell her that she is safe, loved, and the best thing you've ever had a hand in creating because she'll need your support to fall back on when the world knocks her down. Give her the wings to soar, but let her be the one in control of her flight pattern.

How to Encourage Your Daughter to Pursue Her Dreams and Goals

Headstrong daughters are challenging to parent when they are young, but this trait will serve them well in the future. Encourage her endeavors. Put on the brakes whenever the price tag is too high or if there isn't enough time in your family's busy schedule to accommodate extra lessons right now. Just make sure to keep your promises and follow through at the next opportunity so that your daughter knows you are serious—a man of your word instead of someone who provides empty promises and "maybes" that leave holes in her.

Be the guy who tells her what she did is wonderful. Clap for her and cheer the loudest. Gently reassure her, lift her up, and encourage her to take on the world. Your little girl deserves to know that you're in her corner no matter what happens.

If someone comes along and breaks her confidence, you need to repair those gaps by reassuring your daughter that you love her. Nothing is perfect or guaranteed, and we all fall flat on our faces sometimes. It's a normal part of the learning process to fail. But the key to success is never staying down when you're at the bottom. Lift her up, help her stand, and set her on her way again to achieve her goals because she is every bit as capable as completing what she set out to do, even if she stumbled along the way.

The point is that she never gave up. And you didn't either.

You're her first, and should be the loudest, cheerleader. You're the person who will bandage her bruised ego and clean her scrapes when she falls. Like learning to ride a bike, there will be times when the damage doesn't seem worth the effort to get back up and try again. Be the gentle voice of reason: Assure her that it's okay to be afraid. Feel the pain or fear; acknowledge it. Take a breath and let it go. When she's ready to try again, you'll be right there to watch her face her fears, overcome them, and ride on despite what had previously held her back.

Celebrate this tremendous achievement as if it were one of your own because, in a way, it is. You had a hand in creating this amazing human and now you have the privilege to see her blossom into a fearless, confident, incredible, independent, and unique individual.

Other ways to encourage your daughter to succeed in life is to be ever-mindful of how you talk about others, particularly how you express your feelings about other women. If your daughter hears you sexualizing women, she'll learn that appearance and being sexual is how to get a man's attention. You want to say encouraging things to your daughter to make this a non-issue so that she doesn't fall into the "people-pleasing" behaviors that will end in her attracting the wrong kind of partner.

If your daughter hears you talk about women using misogynistic stereotypes like women can't drive, women are only good for one thing, or someone is such a stupid woman, your daughter will internalize these comments, too. She'll begin to wonder if that's how you'll feel about her when she's an adult. Instead, you should be verbalizing when you see a woman who has done something that you would be honored to have your daughter do such as becoming the first female vice president, winning a gold medal in the Olympics, or being the first person in her family to graduate college.

Compliment women for more qualities they possess than how they look or make you feel. Your daughter is an impressionable sponge that wants to make you proud. Make sure you're praising her efforts instead of her thinness or beauty. Those things will fade. As she works through her journey of discovery, help her realize her dreams by giving her ample opportunity to explore books, nature, and all the wonders out there so that she doesn't have to settle for her corner of the world.

When you ask if she had *fun* performing an activity instead of if she won or got first place, you place the emphasis on the process or journey rather than the destination or end result. Life is about how you get where you're going and not just getting through everything else to get somewhere. Your daughter will turn her focus from winning to having fun while learning how to make her dream a reality. This is an important lesson because she won't win all the time. Learning to enjoy the process will help your daughter find a healthy way to deal with disappointment whenever she loses. And that will also teach perseverance so that she doesn't give up on her dreams if they falter or fall through.

Chapter 4
Building Resilience and Coping Skills

Your daughter isn't some delicate flower to be kept in a glass vase on the kitchen counter, but she will still have fragile moments. Treat these moments of being human with care. She may not be fragile like a flower, but if your daughter is fragile like a bomb ready to go off at a moment's notice, treat these tantrums with the utmost care, too.

You'll need to control the storm swirling within yourself to meet her tempestuous tantrum with your cumulative calm. It's the only way to diffuse such a cute twister in the fastest, most efficient way possible. If you don't add fuel to her fiery temper by speaking to her in a calm tone with kind words, she'll have no choice but to try to regulate her overwrought nervous system to meet the calmness of yours.

Calm can be just as contagious as chaotic. Only in these teachable moments, when you are calm, will your child learn the lesson you're attempting to teach or calm down enough to return to her normal activities. Learning how to calm down takes practice.

How to Help Your Daughter Navigate Challenges and Setbacks

There is an anonymous saying that goes, "You cannot see your reflection in boiling water. Similarly, you cannot see truth in a state of anger" (Brown). It is also important to note here that if your child is not in a rational state, or is overstimulated, she will be incapable of receiving the words you're trying to have her listen to. This relates to if she's screaming over something being taken away and you're trying to explain that she cannot play with it because it will hurt her. Or if she's overtired, she may also be unable to settle herself.

In these times of high-stress tantrums, it's best to remove the child from her environment so that the change of place interrupts her current flow. Her brain will recognize the difference as a kind of do-over, a fresh page so-to-speak. Transitions from one room to another, or from the store to the car, gently forces the brain to restart its thinking process—the train it was already on—to move in a different direction as it interprets its new surroundings.

This will, in turn, trigger a calming of the nervous system so that your little one is able to focus on you instead of her very big feelings at the moment. Big emotions can be overwhelming for your child and for you to manage. Taking the interaction elsewhere also gives you a moment between conflict and cool down to settle your high-stress reaction, too.

If you can instigate a kind of reset for you both, you and your daughter will learn to regulate your nervous systems to maintain a much healthier way of handling conflict. To be honest, conflict is an inevitable part of life: The sooner you provide your daughter the tools to navigate it without escalating the conflict to a fever pitch where people get hurt, the better.

Strategies for Teaching Your Daughter Coping Skills and Emotional Regulation

To a little heart that hasn't experienced loss, taking away a toy or perceived "treasured" item, is loss. The best way to handle these intense episodes is to hold your daughter so that it provides full-body deep pressure. This tells her nervous system that it's safe to return to a less excited state. Take care to keep your face pointed away from flailing arms and also watch out for those legs and feet!

But to hold your child with great care conveys an unwavering love that you have for them. Help your daughter to learn that disappointment is inevitable but that the pain of loss will become easier to carry over time. Loss doesn't become easier, we just grow strong enough to carry it with practice. Being there for her, showing her that you understand, helps your daughter carry her emotions better than if she were left to battle these confusing new sensations and situations on her own. She doesn't have to grapple with the failure of trial and error alone because she has you.

Another tactic to deploy when your daughter is a little older is to help her become more aware of her body processes and why she reacts the way she does: Teach her to breathe.

Breathing may seem like a natural function, but strategic and measured breathing can actually work to calm you (and your child) enough to approach any situation more rationally. Start by taking five deep, slow breaths in before you slowly release it. Teach your daughter to join you, turn it into a game by hissing the air out between your teeth like a snake.

If you get her giggling, with the additional help of measured breathing, the natural mix of increased oxygen and endorphins released through laughter will turn the corner in your daughter's tantrum. With enough practice, patience, and consistency, you and your child will train her via emotional regulation how to calm her nervous system rather than continuing in an amped-up, agitated state. By the end of five breaths, you and your daughter should feel more centered, calm, and collected—ready to face the next phase.

Set your expectations to where your daughter is at currently in her emotional development. You may have heard the myth that girls mature faster than boys. This is untrue no matter what your elders have told you. Don't fall prey to this misconception. The truth is that a higher degree of expectation has been placed on female children by societally-structured gender roles and the notion that girls are inferior. A boy is just as capable of understanding the repercussions of his actions and being held accountable for his outburst or bad behavior as any girl.

If your daughter comes home from school in tears because the boy behind her snapped her bra strap, console her. But notify the school immediately that your daughter has been a victim of sexual harassment. It's not on her to be responsible for the misguided, sexual wanderings of her peers or others despite dress code stipulations being more restrictive to what a girl is not permitted to wear than to what boys can. Schools tend to label spaghetti straps, visible bra straps, and short garments as a classroom "distraction" while affording no such restrictions for male-oriented clothing.

Please don't inform your daughter that the boy behaved this way because he "likes her." Abuse in any form is not something to celebrate. And teaching your child that this kind of attention is acceptable and implies "love" is only setting her up to accept dangerous attention and affection mixed with violence that could end in tragedy.

45

Instead, you should arm your daughter with the knowledge that she has every right to firmly state, "No, I don't like when you touch me like that." She only needs to verbalize her boundary a single time. She's informed the other person of the boundary, and that is warning enough if they choose to continue for her to do next what she needs to do to protect herself if she feels threatened or in danger.

She should also know that it is perfectly legal for her to meet the same level of infringement with her own equal action as a way to protect herself. Your daughter has the right to defend herself to the same degree, that is using the same force or method, of the action being placed upon her.

For instance, if a classmate were to snap your daughter's bra strap, she is within her rights to swat the classmate's hand away. She should also interrupt the entire class regardless of if there is a test being administered or lecture being given and inform the instructor right away of what has occurred. Her safety is more important than anything else going on at that moment, and your daughter shouldn't be made to feel like she should keep her abuser's actions a secret just because it "interrupts" others. It wasn't her behavior that caused the interruption. It was the sexual harassment that the other classmate instigated first that caused the interruption.

She may fear repercussion from the student or derision from the class or even a harsh punishment from the teacher, but she will have done what is right to stand up for herself so that any witnesses could give their side of the incident to the teacher, too, and that she protected herself by telling others what happened as soon as it happened.

Your child should never be ashamed or punished for telling the truth. Even if she kicked over an entire can of paint onto your newly-installed hallway carpet, praise her for telling you quickly so that something can be done about it. This way, if something unthinkable happens to her, your daughter will feel safe instead of anxious to seek help. Calmly handle intense situations as best as you can and your daughter will learn from the best how she should do the same.

The Importance of Self-Care for Both Fathers and Daughters

You matter every bit as much as everyone else that you take care of in your life. The best way you can take care of your family is to take care of yourself. It's not always realistic to expect you to be perfect when handling the affairs of others, so try to keep yourself fed, energized, and ready at a moment's notice for times that require superhuman qualities.

To keep your emotions in check during high-conflict conversations, it is best to make sure you're at your peak performance before you enter the "battle arena." You can do this by getting enough sleep (usually eight hours of sleep is recommended), eat three healthy meals each day, participate in some form of physical activity to get your body moving, and engage in activities that make you happy. To be a well-rounded person who doesn't snap because they're suffering from chronic pain or lack of sleep, it's best to get these adverse circumstances under control.

Get a yearly check-up with your doctor to ensure you're physically fit. Like taking a car to a mechanic whenever the check-engine light turns on, if you're driving with all hazard lights blazing, you'll run yourself into the ground, out of gas in no time. Take all the time you need to ensure your health is taken care of (this can be physical health, mental health, and even your emotional health, too).

Perhaps you and your daughter can go to your yearly physicals with your doctors around your birthdays as a reminder to get this important maintenance check each year.

Checking in with your doctor is only one piece of the self-care puzzle. Set aside daily down time for yourself to do something you enjoy, something that is of personal importance to you. This can be as simple as playing a video game before you go to bed, watching a favorite TV show, reading, or enjoying a beer on your back porch. You can choose to include your little one so that she can grow to appreciate the finer things in life that bring you peace, or you can simply exist for a few moments to recenter and ground yourself. You are better able to handle the complexity of life's chaotic moments when you are refreshed than if you let yourself get run down.

Encourage your daughter to enjoy moments of her own solitude. Quiet time spent coloring, playing a video game by herself, going outside to catch fireflies, and listening to music will teach her to be more introspective, contemplative, and help her understand herself better. Menial tasks help us quiet our minds so that we can gather our thoughts, sorting them out by separating them from the loud expectations of everyday life.

There should be time for each of you to spend time together and also apart, both in quiet and in the chaotic fun of vacations, extracurricular activities, and the hustle and bustle of work, school, and family life. Try to make it all count, but don't beat yourself up if all your plans don't go "according to plan." The most important part is to stay present, fully feeling each moment. We cannot emphasize enough the importance of snapping mental pictures of your child as they enjoy their fleeting childhood with all its wonder, discovery, uncertainty, challenges, and victorious achievements that help your daughter soar to new heights. She'll only be this age once, and never this young again. The same principle goes for you, too.

Savor every moment as it exists and give yourself grace as you navigate each new phase of your life as a person, a parent, and an incredibly crucial influence in your daughter's life.

Chapter 5
Navigating Gender Roles and Stereotypes

Strict separation of the sexes never provides advantages. In fact, these polarities tend to take advantage of one group to the improved status of the other. To avoid instilling these archaic values in your daughter, you would be wise to engage in activities like washing dishes, sweeping, vacuuming, cleaning laundry, and showing her how to clean, cook, and provide for herself so that she doesn't have to rely on anyone else for these basic needs to be met.

She would, of course, also benefit from learning how to play baseball as this strengthens eye-hand coordination. Learning how to change a car tire is another basic skill she will likely use in the future that will ensure she is never stranded, helpless.

If your child has smaller hands even as an adult, this never means she is weaker or less capable of completing masculine tasks. It just means that she may need to make adjustments to get the job done, but she is still incredibly capable of completing it to the same level as her male counterparts. Your daughter needs to know that you believe the same: That you believe in her and her abilities. She measures up to any man.

The Impact of Gender Roles and Stereotypes on Girls' Self-Image and Potential

It is incredibly difficult to explain how each person feels, is made to feel, and how it is determined if these subtitles in treatment affect individual outcomes, beliefs, biases, and insecurities. In general, it is safe to say that at some point in your daughter's life, she will experience moments of negative self-image, discouragement from enjoying something or the company of someone for various reasons as deemed by societal pressures, and self-doubt. Your daughter will probably earn less income than her male counterparts and she will more likely than not be the parent who puts her career on hold to bear and rear children.

These are all factors that contribute to your daughter's existence as a female in a world dominated by male policies, workforce, and an overall mentality that promotes the importance of masculinity over the distaste for femininity unless it serves a male-driven purpose. This is not to say that being a man or male is a negative or "bad" thing, but the reality speaks volumes to the prevalence of these kinds of social constructs that will affect your daughter in some way (probably in numerous ways) at some point in her life as a woman.

She will lose a job to someone who is not pregnant or incapable of becoming pregnant just because she would require time off and most employers are not very understanding about their employees taking the necessary time off to care for themselves or others. Capitalism thrives only when its worker "bees" complete their collective work at their assigned posts in the name of keeping the economy going.

Your daughter may find herself in the unfathomable position of needing someone to believe her experience, that she was assaulted or abused, only to discover that she has to relive the events repeatedly as she tells police officers, hospital workers, lawyers, judges, and others what happened. She will be shamed by these people she runs to for help. She will probably not be believed or feel vindicated. The awful truth is that your daughter has a higher probability of being assaulted at some point in her life (greater than a 50% chance) than she does of causing a car accident (with roughly 42% probability) (Malman, 2022; *Quick facts about sexual assault in America—2023*, 2022).

From 1,000 sexual assault cases in the U.S., 975 of these criminals will walk away with no repercussions, serve no jail time, and never be held accountable for their repugnant actions (*The criminal justice system: Statistics*, 2023). And these are only the cases that are reported, where arrests are made, and cases are tried by a court of law. Most rapes and abuse are perpetrated by someone who knows the victim and so the person who is violated often won't report these heinous crimes to autorities because they fear repercussion, retaliation, or death.

It's certainly not a topic that anyone enjoys discussing, but it is still something that will probably impact your daughter's quality of life. No one should ever endure even a modicum of abuse. There is no tolerable amount of abuse to be had and it is untrue that what doesn't kill us makes us stronger. Most people just grow strong enough to carry the heavy burden placed upon them. It creeps up at inopportune moments and haunts even the happiest of moments.

For instance, according to Child Welfare Information Gateway (2019) "abuse or neglect may stunt physical development of the child's brain and lead to psychological problems, such as low self-esteem, which could later lead to high-risk behaviors, such as substance use" and affect nervous system regulation along with creating cognitive and academic issues, too. Abuse leaves behind more than any physical damage that can be seen. The lasting effects of abuse linger and impact the victim indefinitely throughout every stage of their lives even if the abuse stops and is in the past. A single, scarring instance of trauma can derail an otherwise perfectly healthy person forever.

Even walking from a store to the parking lot can become treacherous if someone with nefarious intentions is watching your daughter, waiting to strike. Most men don't have to take extra steps to ensure their personal safety when on a date—that someone might put any kind of drug in their drink or force them to engage in violating, painful, and dangerous entanglements.

For most men, when they have a bad date, the worst that happens is they leave with a bruised ego. Most women fear violent reactions to any rejection. You might notice her laughing at things that she otherwise wouldn't find funny just to deflect any negativity and diffuse an uncomfortable situation. Keeping her date's ego intact instead of risking violent backlash, verbal abrading, or worse becomes something your daughter will probably have to keep in the back of her mind when she's old enough to take on the dating scene.

To be brutally honest, your role as a father is to protect your daughter (mostly) from other men. There is nothing else on the planet you need to prepare her for more than how to defend herself against unwanted advances, uninvited touch, inappropriate comments about her abilities and appearance, being minimized, and being abused.

To strengthen your bond with your little girl, you could participate in a parent-child karate, self-defense course, or boxing class. Physical activity will keep you both fit and healthy. This time together will also give you both a sense of community, to reinforce your confidence in your abilities. And it will give her the physical, muscle-memory "how-to" moves she needs to protect herself from physical harm.

As your daughter moves up in proficiency, she will gain greater self-esteem. She will also learn more about you as you spend more time together. Use the drive to and from practices to engage in personal storytelling so that your daughter gets to know you. On the opposite way to or from practice, get to know your daughter. Utilize every second with her to its fullest.

Tell your daughter when she does something impressive. Use words that tell her she's capable, intelligent, funny, admirable, unique, and that you are incredibly proud of her. Formulate all your compliments around her and her abilities instead of fleeting characteristics like her appearance like she's pretty, she's fast, or she's better than her peers. These achievements are based on competitive characteris that will fade. No one is always beautiful throughout their entire life, and your daughter won't always be the fastest or strongest competitor. Your daughter will put unnecessary stress on herself to perform or appear like the epitome of perfection. And this will cause other complications like eating disorders, overexertion, feelings of inadequacy, setting unrealistic expectations, fear of failure, depression, and self-depreciation.

Make sure you emphasize that she has fun above placing first or being "the best." Life isn't about the end result but enjoying the journey along the way. Rigid gender roles tend to side with the notion that boys are going to be boys and girls will take care of the home, the family, the food, and everything "not fun." Don't close your daughter into that suffocating box. Help her shatter societal expectations by being the loudest feminist dad ever—feminism isn't a dirty word like you might have been taught it is.

Feminism isn't "women are better than men," instead it means that all genders are equal and deserve equal opportunity to achieve the same things in life, to live as equals in all areas of existence, and to maintain a more egalitarian approach instead of "men do this and women just can't because they're the weaker sex or are too emotional" to handle it. No one has had to fight for "men's rights" but you can be on the frontlines of advocating that your daughter have access to every right that you've been probably not given a second thought to such as body autonomy, applying for a credit card, having a job outside the home, or being able to vote.

It's important to take all of these challenges that women face into consideration as you raise your daughter in a highly volatile society where she will constantly battle others (primarily male lawmakers) telling her what she can and cannot do just because she was born a girl. You can vote like your daughter's future depends on it because, in all honesty, it does until she is of age to vote for her rights herself.

Strategies for Promoting Gender Equality and Challenging Stereotypes

Equality is *not* giving everyone the same opportunity to learn the same information in school or giving them all the same foods to eat. True equity is giving each individual what they need to thrive and succeed. The necessities may be different for each person because physiology, cognition, and physical disparities may impede a person's ability to make the most of the standard assistance or opportunity given to most individuals.

It's also crucial to note that social systems exist in the U.S. and various other countries that further impede individuals who belong to minority group's ability to live a normal, successful life without having to navigate additional red tape, hoops to jump through, and steps to take to achieve the same outcome as someone who is not part of a minority group. Just because discrimination (or different treatment dependent upon preconceptions and prejudice) doesn't happen to you doesn't mean that it doesn't exist or isn't a problem.

Ways you can help build your daughter up are to educate her. Encourage her curious nature. Let her discover her environment, her abilities, and help her learn to use her voice to speak up. Telling her to quiet down, calm down, or stop being so dramatic when she's trying to communicate with you will do the exact opposite of building her up.

If you find your daughter wound up and you're having difficulty keeping up with her, take a deep breath yourself. Keep eye contact as you help her breathe, too. Use a calm voice to say, "Take a deep breath, think about what you're trying to tell me, and try again so that I can understand."

No person in the history of humanity has ever calmed down by being told to "calm down." So we need to try a different tactic. Be the calmness you're trying to evoke from your daughter. Teach her to regulate her responses when she is overexcited so that when she is faced with adversity as an adult, she is able to stand her ground.

Encourage your daughter to stand up for herself. The more you use phrases she can easily repeat when she needs them, the more she will speak up. You can tell her it's appropriate to say, "I disagree," or "That's not what I remember happening," and "I don't like that, please stop." Tell her often and emphatically that "no" is a complete sentence and should only have to be said once. Any more than that, and she has every right to walk away from the situation to protect herself.

The more you treat your daughter like an equal instead of seeing her as "just a girl," the more she will learn from you that she is capable of anything and everything—that nothing holds her back, not even her gender.

The Importance of Modeling Healthy, Respectful Relationships

This part of parenthood cannot be stressed enough: Be mindful that your child is continuously watching everything little thing you say, do, don't do, or don't say regardless of how trivial you may think what you're doing is. She's always watching. Choose your words and actions accordingly: Is this something you wouldn't want your child to witness you doing? Would you think poorly of your daughter if she were to do the exact same thing you're doing now? How would it make her feel to know that you might not make the same choice you expect her to make?

It's best to be consistent in your respectful treatment of each person you meet or have contact with so that your daughter adopts this fundamental, universal way of approaching every interaction with respect regardless of any number of demographics or social definitions that could divide humans into separate categories such as class, race, gender, abilities, and appearance.

Showing the same courtesy to someone who irritates you as you would to someone you wish to impress will go a long way in modeling the type of behaviors and manners you wish to see your daughter use. Engage in polite, professional conversations. You can tell your daughter afterward that that was difficult for you to do, but you still chose to do what is right instead of what felt easy.

Furthermore, you should demonstrate equality within your relationships with others by ensuring that you participate in both giving and receiving (otherwise known as compromising) in equal measure. Express honest concerns when you get too little in return or feel stuck or lied to. Let your daughter see you apologize or atone for mistakes. It's also good for her to see you amicably accept an apology from others, too. This helps build on the principle that individuals possess free will (or choices that they alone are responsible for making) and that reciprocation is expected, but so is speaking up for yourself when you feel slighted.

Another great way of instilling patience and humility in your child is to remain slow to judge situations and others unfairly without considering all the evidence. Don't jump to conclusions but rather give the benefit of the doubt that your first impression is *not* the *only* explanation. Allow your daughter enough grace to approach you first, to express her reasoning or explain. Often our assumptions are wrong because there are an infinite number of possibilities for any given situation. Context helps elucidate any misconceptions we've concocted ourselves, but when you assume the worst it tends to make a bad situation worse.

You don't want to risk losing a loving, lasting relationship with your daughter over something as flimsy as made-up information. Like when she was little, and you chased away monsters that frightened her, you need to let your child assuage your fears with the truth.

Make sure that she knows you love her, accept her for who she is and not for who you thought she would be or who you want her to be. She is always your little girl, but she's her own person first and foremost. Any relationship requires sacrifice, accountability, and perseverance. And though you may not always agree with your daughter's choices, she will see how hard you try to understand her as long as you keep trying, keep talking to her.

In her teen years, your daughter will seek or attract and accept relationships with others as abusive or mutually respectful. Perhaps she will even enter into a mix of both types of relationships. Her success at staying away from abusive relationships will largely depend on how she sees the relationships work or fail in her family—primarily in your relationship with her mother. If she witnesses huge blow-ups, no conflict resolution, and resentment building until someone storms out then she will become desensitized to these kinds of unhealthy altercations and learn no productive ways to cope or navigate conflict satisfactorily.

However, when she sees both the conflict and the resolution, your daughter learns that confrontation and accountability are not things to run away from but rather they are a normal part of life. She will observe how you and your partner reconcile your differences and learn to work together again to solve problems.

Seeing how you work well with others will teach your child the tools she needs to work with others in her life, too. She will pick up phrases from you that she sees work to get the ball rolling toward progress again. If you say, "I'm sorry for my part of the argument; let's work together to finish dinner and clean up," then you're teaching your daughter that everyone is allowed to be wrong. She will also see the value in making a bad situation right again—fixing what was broken.

You can also throw out praise instead of criticism because studies have shown that productivity increases when positive observations are conveyed rather than informing someone of what they're doing wrong (Corpus and Good, 2021). Stating the negative feels demeaning and the person on the receiving end usually slows production because they may decide that there's no use in doing more when they were doing their best and it wasn't good enough. On the flipside, if you commend the person for something they're doing right, then they are more likely to continue working at the same level of production as before. You may even see them pick up the pace with renewed motivation to do more to earn more praise.

The old adage goes that you catch more flies with honey than you do vinegar, and there is some truth to that. Try to keep this in mind as you deal with conflict, everyday interactions to make them positive, and as you choose to whom or to what you allocate your attention to if it will be your family or something else. Take time for your needs and for work obligations, but think of your family first when considering every choice and how it will affect them. Could you make a better choice?

Most healthy relationships boil down to mutual respect, interest, and effort to stay in contact with one another. This applies to when your daughter is young and especially when she grows up to chase her dreams. When you put in the effort to respect others, including your daughter, she will invite you along on her journey through life. She won't forget any of the life lessons you've taught her.

Certain phases that are natural to the ebb and flow of life, and circumstances that may seem beyond your control right now, feel overwhelming. Your perseverance will pay off in the end. Hang in there. It gets better and you will be rewarded for your efforts and tactful way you handle your daughter's heart by being ever-mindful of what you say and how you say it.

Chapter 6
Talking About Sex and Relationships

It's completely understandable to feel uncomfortable discussing sexual matters and relationship advice with your daughter. She still needs to know that you are willing to listen to her regardless of the topic she's seeking your input about and that you are in her corner at all times. Look at these vulnerable moments as a manifestation of all the hard work you've put in to show your daughter that you are a person worthy of her trust.

Keeping a respectful tone and genuine interest in anything she's discussing with you will convey that her feelings matter *to you*. You'll need this advantage in the awful event that something transgressive happens to her like sexual abuse, assault, or rape and she needs to confide in you. Help her feel safe. She needs to know that you are a non-judgemental person to run to in times of need. She needs to know that you believe her; and that you believe *in* her.

Laying the groundwork now by engaging with your daughter, actively listening to her, and taking an interest in the things that interest her will give you the advantage of being the shoulder she will trust to cry on whenever her world falls apart.

How to Have Open, Honest Conversations With Your Daughter

Your voice may break, your cheeks might get red with embarrassment, and you may wring your hands until you find the courage to look your daughter in the eye, but you will get through this. Even the most uncomfortable conversations about taboo topics means that your daughter trusts you and has given you her utmost respect to discuss such a secretive yet significant subject that affects everyone's life at some point—sex.

There is no need to go into great detail about anything right off the bat, but keep an open mind when your daughter approaches you with her probably deeply premeditated phrasing about anything that is so personal to her. She's rehearsed these words in her head over and again until the distress of living in uncertainty brought her to you. You should feel honored that your daughter trusts you so implicitly.

Match your choice of details with her age so that she isn't overwhelmed with information before she has more context for the next big topic. Let her ask questions and answer them honestly by using the correct anatomical terms. This will help her identify any abuse if she is touched inappropriately. Using accurate anatomical words for body parts will also empower your daughter to take ownership of her body instead of fearing it or being ashamed of it. She deserves to feel at home in her own skin.

By shying away from answering uncomfortable questions, you might inadvertently imply that her body is "dirty," her feelings are "wrong," or that she is responsible for any lustful feelings someone else might be having about her or her changing body. Your daughter needs to be reassured that each person's feelings, actions, and words are their own responsibility regardless of anything else they may see that they want to possess. Teach her, too, that "no means no—the first time." She is not "dirty" if she is desirable, but it would be a good idea to wait to engage in more intimate forms of love when she and her partner are both mature and ready to handle possible consequences of whatever choice they make. It's imperative to note that consent is not always a part of these intimate encounters.

Consenting to have sex does not imply consent to become pregnant or become a parent. Purity culture, or putting the emphasis on being a virgin/pure before marriage, goes hand-in-hand with rape culture in that the blame for sexual violence is often erroneously placed on the victim (most of the time the victim is female) instead of the perpetrator for their choice of infractions and heinous taking of what was never theirs to possess of another person.

The subject matter becomes a bit heavy here because you should know that your daughter will probably have to face many instances where her boundaries are tested, crossed, or completely violated. Whether she is coerced with words or physical force, your daughter is going to be under a tremendous amount of pressure to be submissive or accommodating toward those she perceives to be authority figures based upon the boundaries you set for her now. Check your priorities often in what you're teaching your daughter to obey, if she is taught to be timid and tolerant or confident and courageous.

Strategies for Teaching Healthy Boundaries and Consent

"When you were never fed love on a silver spoon, you learn to lick it off knives" is a cautionary lyric from the band Voila about how crucial it is to be your child's first, most stable unconditional love relationship (Quinn, Eisner, and Ross, 2022). The insight here is to offer your child constant, reliable affection each and every time they toddle over seeking your attention. The haunting implication from not doing so is that your little girl will grow into a young woman who is willing to accept any amount or form of love because that craving for acceptance was never provided to her when she was a child.

A sure way to prevent crossed boundaries becoming acceptable in your daughter's life is to set boundaries yourself. Model respect towards your child's mother, your child, and others you interact with on a daily basis. Employ your manners like telling a stranger "thank you" for keeping the door open for you or open the door for the stranger behind you. Saying "please" and "thank you" are only the beginnings of teaching good manners.

You can even help your daughter draw boundaries that make her comfortable with other family members. If she doesn't want to give Aunt Sally a hug or let Grandpa kiss her on the mouth, she shouldn't have to submit in order to save face or avoid an argument. When your daughter shakes her head, back her up. You can simply attest that your daughter isn't comfortable hugging just yet. Maybe they could try a high five or fist-bump instead until a more meaningful connection is established.

Family members that your daughter doesn't see on a daily basis are a kind of "stranger" to her. Forcing her to hug, kiss, or accept such intimate physical contact with someone she doesn't know sets a dangerous precedent that "daddy says it's okay for strangers to treat me this way." And so, she may be more inclined to follow the unscrupulous instructions a stranger with worse intentions demands she obey.

If you don't support your daughter or show her how important she is to you, she will continually search for that validation in others. This is a dangerous game. Pieces of your daughter will be left in the hands of villainous monsters and she will break along the cracks your inattention left in her childhood dreams. Be the glue that holds her together; be part of her life.

So many missed opportunities leave your daughter vulnerable to predation by vile individuals who excel at finding something good and breaking it for the fun of masterminding the destruction—lording power over an inferior, vulnerable puppet that falls into their trap baited with promises of love and stability.

These are all the areas of your daughter's life that you are in charge of fulfilling and stabilizing. If you don't take note, make the effort, and make time for your little girl, this will be the cycle her life follows. It's a never-ending roller coaster of ups and downs too heavy for her to carry alone without the tools you need to give her to avoid this detriment altogether. Here's how:

To Consent Is to Express a Consistent, Enthusiastic "Yes"

When discussing the concept of "consent" with your daughter, it's best to start out using a simple explanation. Consent can be shown in asking her if she wants to give you a hug or if it's okay to give her a kiss on the cheek. Let your daughter learn to say "yes" or "no." Don't get upset when she denies you access to her personal space.

She needs to learn that only she has the power to grant or deny access to her and everything that is personal to her.

Exercises help build confidence. Giving your daughter ample opportunities to practice saying "no" and to set her boundaries will engrain in her that "no" means "no" and that only "yes" gives the "green light" to proceed. Anything other than an enthusiastic "yes" is also a hard "no," and shouldn't be seen as a challenge to convince her to ultimately concede and say "yes." Tell your daughter, make sure she understands, that coercion (wearing someone down until they feel like they have to agree just so that the other person will stop harassing her) is also unacceptable.

She needs to tell you immediately if that ever happens to her. You can gently tell your daughter that she will feel like something is uncomfortable if she's not ready, or never wants to partake in an activity. Her body will send signals that alert her. These can be described as "butterflies in the tummy" or a fluttering feeling. She might feel her heart beat faster, her breathing quicken, and she might feel sweaty or panicky. If she ever feels like she's in danger or afraid, your daughter should try her hardest to run, scream, kick, fight back, and make it as difficult to carry her away as she can.

It's a cruel, unfair world in which we live. Prepare your daughter to face the real possibility that she should constantly be aware of her surroundings, never go somewhere alone with anyone she doesn't know, and never talk to strangers. If she needs to use the public restroom, you should wait outside the door for her to return or have her go with a family member to use the restroom. It is harder to kidnap two people than just a single, small girl.

Something else to discuss with your daughter is that consent works both ways. Explain that if someone tells your daughter "no" or "stop" that she should also stop what she is doing that is crossing someone else's boundaries. Everyone has their own boundaries and comfort zones and these can vary greatly from person to person. It's always better to ask permission than to beg for forgiveness. The power of open communication helps prevent any confusion about where boundaries begin and consent can commence.

The Importance of Promoting Body Positivity and Self-Love

An innumerable amount of times throughout a single day, your daughter will have doubts. Doubts about her appearance, her worth, her ability, her safety, her intelligence, her weight, her life choices, and many other areas of her physical, professional, romantic aspects of her life. She will worry that she doesn't measure up to societal expectations. Her own expectations may feel overwhelming. Making enough money while balancing her family and work life may feel impossible. She'll wonder if she's made a mistake. She'll tell herself that she's "ugly" or "worthless" and that she isn't what she's been led to believe is the "ideal woman."

She might question taking a second plate of food at dinner because her friends are thinner than she is. Dangerous diet fads, forcing herself to throw up after a meal, using laxatives to lose weight, or excessively and obsessively exercising are all dangers most young girls (and even some boys) face primarily during adolescence.

Puberty is an awkward time of significant change in a child's life. Children develop at different rates, some more rapidly than others in areas such as height, weight, acne, muscle mass, breast tissue, and dental disparities like needing braces, a retainer, or having wisdom teeth surgery. Every aspect of a child's life during fifth grade into college sets them apart from their peers in both favorable and embarrassing ways.

It's your job as a father to help your child make this transition into their adult body as seamless as you possibly can. But you should know that no one is going to get it right every single time. You can't shield your daughter from ever being bullied or believing she is imperfect. That's just not realistic.

But what you can do is be as encouraging as possible. Spend time with your daughter when she gets home from school and especially on the weekends so that she has time to express her concerns. Studies have shown that the time of day a teen is most likely to confide in you about anything troubling or important is in the late evening hours once dinner is finished (Wisner, 2021). One reason for this is that they might be having trouble quieting their minds before bed and what's on their mind is too heavy for them to face alone, so they turn to you.

Even if you're exhausted, don't let it show because this could be a pivotal opportunity to help your child and get to know what's going on in their world. Your daughter's world is more quiet at night with academic and home expectations being resolved by this time of day.

It's important to give your daughter the reins in this situation to lead the conversation. Ask a few open-ended questions if you must. The more she talks, the more in-depth the conversation will get. You'll be surprised how candid your child will become after even a few minutes of midnight conversation. It's okay to relax bedtime curfews for the sake of getting to know your child better.

Offer affirmations, words of wisdom, and gentle reminders that you're available to listen or to help if she needs you at any point.

Chapter 7
Supporting Your Daughter Through Adolescence and Beyond

Long past are the toddler days when your daughter's needs made sense. If she was hungry, you would feed her. If she needed a diaper change, that was easy enough to complete, too. Now, she has friends at school, homework, and access to social media and a cell phone to connect with her peers. It gets complicated, but be understanding that there are real reasons behind mood swings and outbursts. We'll help you better understand what emotions fuel these rapid changes in temperament and what you can do to help yourself, and your child, navigate them.

Strategies for Supporting Your Daughter Through the Challenges of Adolescence

One of the biggest changes you will probably become aware of is when your daughter starts her first period. Treat these sensitive, sometimes alarming changes in your daughter's mood, her perception of herself, and how she reacts in any given situation like you would if you're trying to figure out why your newborn baby is crying. Does it hurt? Can you do anything to help ease the pain like giving her a pain reliever like Tylenol or Midol? Sometimes, placing a heating pad over the lower abdomen set on its lowest heat setting will help ease the intensity of the cramps she's experiencing.

Even though this is a "woman's arena" you can still take interest in your daughter. Know the kind of sanitary pads she prefers—this includes size, wings or no wings, degree of absorbency, and keep your bathroom well-stocked. It should not be viewed as emasculating to purchase pads or tampons for your child any more than ringing up an entire case of toilet paper is embarrassing. It's all just a normal, natural part of human life.

Bleeding is not dirty, but it can be messy. If your daughter's mother is unavailable when your daughter has her period, starts her period, or is having her first period, try to remain calm. Your daughter will take her cues from you about how you perceive periods, and her needs, from you. If you say insensitive comments like, "Ew! Gross! I don't want to touch that!" your daughter will begin to feel ashamed that she's "dirty," that having a period every month for roughly a week at a time, is something to feel insecure about even when she has no control over when, how long, or how messy her period will be.

You changed this child's poopy diapers and cleaned up her vomit. You've probably touched her blood at some point before her monthly menstruation occurs, so please try to be understanding. This time in your daughter's life hurts. It's an inconvenience for her, too. She has to worry about her peers seeing the back of her jeans if she bleeds through her pad. Even though most pads stick onto the underwear, with vigorous walking like from class to class or during strenuous activity like in gym class, pads will move away from their original position and bleeding through clothing occurs within minutes.

Other children in her class who don't have as supportive a parent as you are going to call attention to anything they perceive to be a weakness, and they will make fun of your daughter if they notice blood on her clothing. Help your daughter prevent this from happening as much as you can by helping her be prepared.

Once cyclic menses begins, it can take several years for a person to be able to (sort of) predict when a period might be looming. The best way to anticipate a pending period is to keep track on a calendar when bleeding starts, each day the bleeding continues, and also mark down the final day of menstruation. You should be able to see a pattern emerge such as an average 28-day cycle (the number of days can vary) that includes the follicular phase when a few eggs begin to mature in the ovaries and uterine lining begins to thicken in preparation for a fertilized egg to implant. Ovulation then occurs (when a single mature egg is released by the ovaries and makes its way through the fallopian tubes into the uterus—the egg is only viable for 48 hours) and is part of the luteal phase. Menstruation follows if the egg does not meet sperm (fertilization), which signals the end of the reproductive cycle for someone who has a uterus.

This is a lot of information, and you probably don't want to think of your little girl as having a reproductive system at all. We completely understand and are sympathetic. However, you must understand that whether you want to acknowledge the existence of this part of your daughter's life or not, it will affect her in various ways throughout her entire life. She doesn't have the option to ignore what goes on with her body, so we sincerely encourage you to keep an open mind and to listen to your daughter whenever she says she needs or wants your help, to confide in you about anything affecting her, and especially to listen in earnest whenever she has an issue as she looks to you to for help.

How to Prepare Your Daughter for Adulthood and Independence

Setting boundaries, realistic expectations, and consequences early on in your child's life is mutually beneficial to you as the parent and to your child. She will realize that rules exist for a reason. No one is above facing the consequences of their choices, and sometimes, those consequences have lasting effects.

Prepare your daughter to face the world by giving her real-world expectations. Help her learn how to clean, prepare a meal, budget a grocery list, and give her a reasonable allowance for her age when she completes chores each week so that she can learn the value of money. Teach her how to save money, how to spend it wisely, and how to grow her skill set so that she can earn more by giving her a variety of tasks to complete.

Never limit her to only learning society-based, gender-assigned tasks like washing the dishes, cleaning the house, vacuuming, mopping, cleaning the laundry, and cooking. She should also learn how to change a tire, how to balance a checkbook, how to throw a baseball and catch it, and how to paint, lay floor tile, and use various tools.

Start your daughter out with her own toy tool kit, building blocks, and cars. Buy her baby dolls, dresses for make-believe, and teapots for tea parties if she's interested in those things, too. The same goes for your child whether they are male or female: Let your child use their imagination with any toys they gravitate to regardless of how *you* feel about them so that they can develop to their full potential.

Give her choices instead of demanding she follow a rigid path you've decided she must follow. When your daughter knows that she can dream, do, and be anything because you believe in her, her entire world will open up with endless possibilities. Nothing will hold her back when *you* have her back. Let her dream, relish in these fleeting moments of innocent childhood wanderings, and marvel at the unique child you've been blessed to parent.

The Importance of Maintaining a Strong, Positive Relationship With Your Daughter Throughout Her Life

To stand the test of time, your relationship with your daughter must contain these three key characteristics: trust, unconditional love, and stability. Remain the same father with the same dad jokes and dole out the same consequences for extreme disobedience. You have to be both "good cop" and "bad cop" depending upon the situation. There are exceptions to every rule, of course, so pick your battles wisely by asking yourself if this will really matter to you as much in five years? If the answer is no—let it go.

You must build upon your daughter's trust as she grows by first making the conscious choice to put her needs first above your own. If you see that she's going to make a debilitating mistake, by all means do everything within your power to prevent her from making it by explaining (in detail) all the ways her actions might play out. In the end, however, the decision to take the path is hers alone.

Mentally prepare yourself for the contingency that she might need you if she's had a lapse in judgment and give her the grace to come back to you as a safe place to recover.

This is your most important job as a father—remain a strong champion of your daughter, to hold your arms out and console her whenever she messes up. Error is part of human nature. It is every child's nature to arrive in the world with fresh curiosity and a naive notion that they are invincible. The world has cruel ways of teaching them to be cautious rather quickly with their first bruises, scraped elbows and knees, and malicious classmates who claim to only tease. These wounds become central to who your child will become.

What also is amalgamated into a child's core memories is your reaction to these wounds. Do you deride or shame? Do you imply it was her fault for being an easy target? Or do you welcome your broken baby bird back into the nest and tell her that it hurts now, but it won't hurt forever. She is going to meet many villains on the way to greatness, but that doesn't mean that she should ever give up or let them win. Encourage her to try again.

You know that she is wonderful, amazing, unique, and every-thing good in this world. Tell her to shine on despite the woefully gloomy clouds who try to snuff out her greatness. Her trust in others begins with her trust in you.

Each time you show up in times of distress, you prove to her that your actions match your words. Of course you love your daughter, but being visible and available is how you *show* her that. You only fail by not putting in the work for your little girl the same as you would throw everything you've got into a crucial work assignment. The only person who will remember every late night you spent at work is your child who felt your absence.

Balancing work and home life may feel like an impossible task, but it is necessary to put your family first often. Your child is only going to be this small, have moments this memorable and life-altering, once in her life so you only have one shot to be part of that or you risk losing out on your daughter looking back on these times with fondness instead of disappointment.

Your encouragement or derision will echo in her mind forever. She'll hear you cheering her on telling her there are no limits on her success. Or, she'll constantly question her abilities if she remembers how she wasn't "good enough," "interesting enough," or "worth" playing dolls with or teaching how to play catch. Your words carry a weight like no other.

Your daughter's idea of who you are will define her throughout her entire life. But luckily for you both: You each have an entire lifetime of opportunities to support one another, learn from and about each other, and enjoy each other's company. Your daughter will change physically throughout the years. She will experience meeting people who challenge the values you've instilled in her. And her perspective will mature accordingly. Respect her at all stages and listen with an open mind as she talks about what she has learned along her journey. Welcome honest conversations that may also challenge what you've learned in life so that you can compare notes. Discourse is healthy for you both.

Humankind is meant to evolve, to learn, make mistakes, and choose how to do better. Being confronted with views you may find in opposition to your beliefs is not meant to start a war within your family. If your daughter has mustered the courage to include you in parts of her life that are of utmost importance or secrecy because she fears she'll let you down or disown her, you should take a step back from who you are to give her the space to talk. Try your best to not jump to conclusions or interrupt her.

"Ruling" from a place of anger or fear doesn't mean you're more respected as a man or a father just because your daughter follows every rule and expectation laid out before her. She may do everything she thinks will earn her praise, but she may be choosing her life path for all the wrong reasons. This creates a "people pleaser" who will end up in relationships with others who expect to use and abuse her.

The best thing you can do for your relationship with your daughter is to be honest about your initial thoughts and feelings. Calmly address your concerns and outcomes you fear will adversely affect her. But, above all, hear her out. For every reason you have why she shouldn't, she may have 20 reasons why she should, needs to, or wants to.

Your daughter may not always be right, and neither may you, but you love her. She'll always be your child—a part of you, someone you helped create, but not necessarily a direct extension of you. She's a separate individual from you who must navigate her life independently from you in a new generation while facing new challenges you've never dreamed existed during your own experience.

It may require several conversations until you each reach a mutual resolution, but make sure that your daughter knows at the end of each interaction that you still love her. Just that— you love her no matter what. Not that you love her, "but" or you love her "if." Just love her without expectation that she must fit into the mold you shaped with rules, remarks about politics, religious consequences taught at church, or prejudices implicit or explicitly conveyed over the course of her life as she watched how you treated others.

Your daughter may think she knows what will disappoint you or cause her to fall out of favor with you because children watch everything their parents say and do. At every chance for reassurance your daughter tests your patience or boundaries, she should still walk away knowing that you still love her. At her worst, you need to hug her, look her in the eye, and even if you're not good with the mushy emotional stuff, you can still express your unwavering appreciation for her being your daughter.

Each time you are there to cheer for or mend your daughter, she will notice. This will build trust. Meeting her where she is, whether it's broken on the ground so that you can lift her back up or gently bringing her back down to reality will also show your daughter that you are in it for the long haul. You are a stable force in her life that she can rely on when the world overwhelms her.

Try with all your strength to be the hero your daughter knows you to be. You are her protector from monsters who would crush her. You are her first teacher in all ways. There will be moments you aren't proud of but you hold the power to mend or to break this tiny person you have invested in since birth. All her hopes hinge on you being pleased with her and what she does. Be the first to apologize when you are wrong or have hurt her and be the first to cheer her on, too. The more you show up and stay focused on your daughter's joy, the more smiles you will share together. All you can do is try, try, try!

Chapter 8
Navigating Life Transitions With Daughters

Transitions are difficult for children, and their parents. Particularly for fathers who have not been in the position of growing up female, the transition from child to teen may be mystifying and confusing. Try not to let this discourage your involvement in your child's life just because you do not understand what she's going through. She still needs you.

Supporting Daughters Through Major Life Transitions (Like Puberty and High School)

There's no doubt that change is inevitable. Change is the only constant in life besides death and taxes. Making these rites of passage more meaningful and less traumatic is, believe it or not, something within your power (at least to some extent).

You can help lessen the embarrassment of when your daughter gets her first period by talking with her a couple years before she begins bleeding. Before you go buying up every feminine hygiene product in the aisle, you should conduct a bit of reconnaissance, do your homework, and buy her a package of maxi pads that are of the correct absorbancy. Absorbancy and size are usually indicated by illustration on the front of the pad package. You should also choose the kind that has "wings" that stick to panties. This feature helps the pad stay in place better.

Choose the lower absorbency and the smaller pad for starters. Once your daughter has started her period and gotten more accustomed to her individual flow, duration, and how well or poorly the pads cover her underwear to prevent embarrassing leakage, you can choose to change the type or brand of pad for the next period.

Encourage your daughter to carry a small purse with at least two pads in case she accidentally drops one and can't use it. It's always better to be prepared than to not have what you need. This is especially true whenever the potential to be mocked or shamed for having a normal bodily function becomes embarrassingly visible to others.

Spare your daughter the surprise of beginning to bleed and her not understanding how this could happen or that it's a natural part of becoming an adult for someone who has a uterus.

Talk to her at every age about her body by assigning the correct anatomical names for body parts, even those that should be kept "private." This is a form of early sex education and it is absolutely appropriate to teach a child about their body even at an early age. In fact, it is an essential way to help protect your child against exploitation. Tell her that she should keep her private parts "private" and that if anyone touches her there, she should tell you or another trusted adult immediately. Your daughter will learn that her body is her own.

When your daughter is a bit older and starts asking you questions such as, "Where do babies come from?" you should be honest with her. Use simple words that she understands and keep the content to exactly what she is asking. You don't need to go into great detail about the nuances of sex, attraction, or exactly how painful childbirth is. Listen to the questions your child asks. Prepare yourself by taking a few breaths before answering.

If you would like to start a conversation to get a sense of what your child knows (or thinks they know about sex), you can ask an open-ended question like, "How do you think babies are made?" At age five, a simple answer of: "Most babies are made when a couple has sex. The baby grows inside a special part of the body called the uterus. After about nine months, the baby is born." You can be as specific or vague as you feel comfortable.

The best course of action is to use the correct terminology to describe the details if your child is mature enough and curious to know more than a general overview. Gatekeeping knowledge usually ends in catastrophic consequences and regret—wishing they'd known how to prevent something lifelong like contracting a sexually transmitted infection (STI) or getting pregnant.

Present your daughter with ample opportunities to learn about her body, how to protect against unwanted pregnancy and STIs, and how to clean herself properly. If you feel too embarrassed to talk to your child directly, you can also check out library books that your daughter can look through on several of these sensitive subjects. Another tactic you may wish to use is to text back and forth any questions or answers so that all pressure is off to discuss taboo topics face to face.

You have the power to prevent unnecessary heartache and embarrassment for your daughter by allowing her unfettered access to your wide breadth of knowledge in all areas.

When she is small, learning to potty train, you tell her she needs to wipe from front to back to prevent her from getting an itchy infection. You teach her how to wash her hair with shampoo and how to rinse it out without getting any stinging residue in her eyes.

As your daughter grows up, she will rely on you less for helping her maintain her hygiene, but you can still be there for her whenever she has questions or needs anything like a new kind of deodorant to cut through her after-gym-class sweat or if she thinks she wants to try tampons instead of pads.

As her parent, you will be her go-to for all things as long as you keep the line of communication open and welcoming.

From Manic Middle School to High-Pressure High School

Middle school is probably going to be a difficult time for your child. It's all awkward phases, physical changes, increased and noticeable body odor, and power struggles between peers who had once been friends. Relationships are changing and school subject matter is getting more complicated.

This chaotic mix of academic pressure and interpersonal upheaval can take its toll on your child and their psyche. Elementary school was exciting—full of exciting field trips, introductions to the amazingly magical world of science, and learning how to read. Around third and fourth grades, the focus shifts from learning how to read to reading to learn. This can be intimidating for a child who struggles with expressive or receptive language cognition.

Other children who have no academic concerns may appear to breeze through coursework like it's second nature, but children have a tendency to mask when they struggle. This type of nonchalantly saying they're "fine" when they're really anxious, upset, or need help is more common in girls than boys (*Children or young people who mask or camouflage their needs*, n.d.).

When that golden moment pops up out of nowhere when your child or teen is settled and seems more willing to talk about what's happening in their isolated, sometimes overwhelming world, take every second to give them your full attention. Hold back questions unless it adds to the conversation in a positive way that prompts your child to divulge more. When your daughter gets going down a "rabbit hole" of sorts, she may be better able to sort out her emotions and concerns enough to elucidate them to you so that you can help her carry her mental load.

You can repeat a statement back to her that she's just said to let her know you're listening. Give her your full attention in a way that is termed "whole-face listening." This is when you turn your face, gaze, and body toward the speaker so that they know you are completely engaged in the conversation instead of only half-hearing what's being said. It is possible to only *hear* what's being said to you rather than actively *listening*.

To help your daughter the most when she's ready to open up to you, sit with her. Turn off any electronics and don't answer any phone calls or texts. Nod every so often so that she can see you are following her part of the conversation.

It probably won't surprise you that your daughter will probably feel more comfortable talking to her peers about sexual or romantic issues, smoking, vaping, using drugs, drinking alcohol, and cheating on school tests than she is talking to you or her mother. This doesn't mean that you shouldn't bring these topics up with her independently.

In fact, the best way to protect your daughter from any of these vices she isn't ready to engage in is to begin conversations early before she is asked to pass a joint at a party or to look at her classmate's paper. Keep the atmosphere light instead of accusatory.

Listen to your daughter first tell you what she knows about said topic (try not to cover all of them in a single setting so that the information is better recalled later). Tell her you will love, support, and help your daughter in the event that she ever needs you. Feel free to caution her about the consequences of engaging in cheating, how she could be expelled.

Discuss the nasty details of STIs, how they sometimes last longer than the relationships that cause such miserable symptoms. Explain that there are emotional and social consequences of having sex as a teen—lasting effects are not limited to the life-changing possibilities like having a baby. Not everyone can be trusted to keep secrets, no matter how many times they tell you that they love you.

In the end, all you can do is give your daughter all the information, run down the long list of could-be's, and let your baby bird waddle out of the nest to make her own choices. You've done everything within your power to protect and educate her, and then you wait. Wait for her to return to tell you how great it all was or that you were right. Help her collect any broken pieces or celebrate with her. The important part is to be there for her whatever, and no matter what, she needs. She'll be so much stronger with your support, knowing that she has a safe place to return when or if she needs you.

Navigating Changes in Family Dynamics and Relationships

As a parent, you don't want any of your children to question if you love them or if the world would be a "better" place without them in it. The incredibly sad reality is that not every parent is able to put aside their personal feelings, beliefs, or pride to make their child their top priority.

There will be times when your child lets you down just like there will also be times where you let them down despite your best efforts. There will be times when you let them down in other ways, too. You're not going to get it right every single time, but as long as you put in the effort to try to understand why something is important to your child and you pay attention, you'll be doing the best you can with what you've got at that moment.

Build upon that every chance you get. Soon, you'll have a wider breadth of knowledge and experience from which to pull no matter what your child throws at you.

If your daughter surprises you by discussing topics you know nothing about, you should realize that this information is not new to your child even if it's a shock to you. Ask your daughter to give you time to adjust. Take the time to read every piece of information you can about the topic before you see or talk to her again so that you are better prepared to have a conversation on her level (just as you did when she was younger and you knew more). There will be times in your daughter's adult life that she has different or more knowledge about things than you do. You should be proud of her for that.

Share what you know and let her walk you through the rest. There will be times, too, that you need to ask your daughter for forgiveness, the same as she will need to ask you, too. This swapping of authority figure and child almost levels out and sometimes becomes an inverted version of the original parent-child dynamic as your daughter becomes an adult. One day, she may even need to care for you as you cared for her. Time is an unstoppable force that humans constantly battle: Do we control time or does time control us?

You may find yourself stuck in remembering your daughter as the little girl in pigtails riding her bike instead of the tall grown-up version she has become. She will challenge your notions on social issues, existential matters that make you uncomfortably aware of the finality of life, moral issues, and other hot-button topics. You'll watch your daughter blossom, but you'll grow older, too.

It's in times of chaos amid trying to ensure everyone has what they need when your daughter is little that you won't feel the passage of time so severely. But one day, you'll notice that the house is a lot quieter. You won't be hustling to get everyone to after-school practices. And you'll be surrounded by framed pictures of your child instead of by her presence. You don't want all that time, all those cherished moments, to stay stuck, tucked into picture frames to be admired.

Instead, you want your home to experience the magic of being alive with your child's presence again, so you will do whatever is in your power to welcome your daughter to come home for a visit as often as she possibly can.

To be a welcoming presence for your daughter, you need to realize that your daughter doesn't go out of her way to choose, dress, behave, or change in ways that she knows will disappoint you or make you angry. Remember that she is an individual who has her own thoughts, feelings, beliefs, and experiences that are completely separate from you or anything you've encountered in your lifetime. You've never grown up during her lifetime to deal with the kinds of issues and pressures prevalent in her everyday activities.

Your daughter is making educated choices for herself that she will need to navigate. The consequences are hers to celebrate or handle if they spiral out of control. Lend a hand if you can, but even if you deeply disagree with her choices, you should remember that they aren't a reflection of you or poor parenting. She's your child. She isn't you.

It can be difficult to separate ourselves as parents from the actions of our children. How could we not feel a sense of disappointment or wondering where we went wrong when we've been in charge of keeping these little souls safe for the first 18 years of their lives?

You should feel reassured that anything your daughter does isn't your fault. The only person who can control her actions is herself. This is the same for you and your actions: Only you decide what course of action you will or won't take. Only you are to blame if it goes wrong and only you can take the credit if it goes right.

Try to empathize with your daughter, put yourself in her position, when she's informing you of any monumental changes in her life. She could change anything about herself than you thought you knew and she would still be the small soul you watch toddle their first steps when they were a baby learning to explore their world.

Throughout any changes in family situations like divorce, declarations of love or change in appearance, birth of siblings or children, or any unexpected deaths in the family, two truths remain unchanged. Your child will always be your child. And you want the best possible outcome for them, always.

Do your best to act according to these two principles. Let your child guide you through their part of any life changes. If you are the person these changes rest with, then try your best to hold your child's hand to walk them through your changes, too. Take it day by day, little by little, before the situation becomes overwhelming. The more overwhelmed you or your child is, the greater the probability either of you will say or do something hurtful that you don't mean.

You want to maintain a strong relationship with your child throughout your lives. The best way to accomplish this is to just keep trying to talk, try to keep in contact, and show up as often as you can to events that matter to her. With an open line of communication flowing both to and from your daughter, you both have every opportunity to address any grievances or questions either of you have so that you can keep trying to work out any misunderstandings or complications in your relationship.

With those out of the way, you'll both feel less encumbered when face-to-face interactions take place. You'll know that you are working through any changes that worry you and your daughter will know that you love her regardless. You want her to thrive and you want her in your life. Listen to her. Show her that she matters to you through your conscientious effort to remain a visible, valuable part of her life whatever that may look like as she grows older.

Preparing Daughters for Independence and Adulthood

The time has come that most parents dread: The day your child turns 18 and becomes (legally) an adult. You may opt to have your child continue to live with you until they acquire a job that provides health benefits like paid time off and health insurance, but you can also let them live with you indefinitely if you choose.

Most states in the U.S. allow children to begin working with a work permit (acquired from their high school) at age 16. They can only work a certain number of hours each week (usually about 10 hours) and must take a break during each shift. This depends on the laws in the state in which you live so you can look them up or talk to your child's guidance counselor at school for more advice.

Instill a reliable work ethic in your child earlier than high school by encouraging them to help you out around the house with daily chores (both in and outside the home). Leave rigid, archaic gender roles out of your decision to enlist your daughter's help in lawn, car, or home maintenance. Teach her to use tools for all areas of the house and how to properly avoid injury while handling sharp or dangerous objects.

A child needs to learn more than what they are given to memorize in school in areas such as reading, writing, mathematics, history, and science. They also require socialization to help them acquire social tools to communicate effectively and express themselves clearly in healthy, appropriate ways.

Children also need to learn how to take care of themselves. Brushing their teeth, maintaining good personal hygiene, preparing food, caring for pets, cleaning up a mess, and putting toys away all combine important skills a person needs in preparation for doing these things on a larger scale without adult assistance. Let them practice often so that these healthy habits become second nature well before it is time for them to perform these tasks on their own as adults.

The foundations you model and lay out for your child to follow now will either become the roadblocks they find themselves up against as adults or, if you give them tools to circum-navigate any roadblocks, your child will find their way more easily. They can negotiate for more money when they're being offered a job if they are raised to be confident and trust in their abilities. Your child knows her worth and so she demands to be compensated for the quality skillset she can provide the company. She won't be derailed by being told "no" when she petitions her employer for a raise, she'll find the research she needs to back up her reasonable request instead.

When we tell our children that nothing is impossible, they will believe it. But when we repeatedly tell our children "no" instead of choosing positive phrases, little by little, it wears down their confidence. To say, "Stop doing that," means little to a child. But telling them to "Sit on the couch. Sit still," encourages them to do the "right" thing, or the action you want them to perform. Then, you should praise them by getting on their eye-level, saying your child's name, and follow with, "Thank you for sitting still. You're doing an awesome job!"

Encouragement builds up where shouting negative words only tears down.

The more you practice using the positive phrasing of whatever instruction you're trying to impart to your child, the easier it will become to build up a resilient kid. She won't take "no" for an answer when "no" stands in her way to greatness. That is to say, when hearing "no" is an absurd response to a reasonable request or an obstacle in her way to success.

Another tool you can use to prepare your daughter for the real world is to be honest with her about how hard life is some-times. Bills, pain, disappointment, not being able to spend your time doing what you love, working more days than you have off, and living up to the expectations of others all have their way of infiltrating the unbridled freedom children believe adulthood to be.

Of course you can eat chocolate cake for breakfast, lunch, and dinner—but the health problems, tooth decay, and weight gain will be the unwanted consequences of doing just that. Adulthood isn't about getting everything you want or doing nothing and getting everything in return. Your daughter will understand this so much better if you set realistic expectations for her by showing her real-life cause and effect.

Budgeting

Give her a small allowance. Let her budget, spend, and save according to her wishes. When she doesn't have the money saved up for an expensive toy she wants, gently explain that you know a way she can afford the toy she wants if she *budgets* her allowance like this: You can explain how you save money or you can use the following model to help her understand how money works.

One example is to use the 50-20-30 model of saving, spending, and using money to achieve a finance goal. Twenty percent of your paycheck or allowance will go directly into savings, never to be touched until you've reached the savings goal. Then, 30% of your income will be directed to "fun" activities or objects so that you don't feel cheated out of doing anything you enjoy. This category is for things your child "wants." You don't want to live to work, the goal is to work to live. And lastly, 50% of your allowance or payday will funnel into your bills and other things you need (like gas, tuition, car payments, repairs, food, healthcare, and the like).

For a child, they may not have many "needs" that you aren't providing for them. But this allotment can go toward lunch money or snacks that are extra. You could also separate allowance categories into gift giving money, savings, snack money, electronics, entertainment subscriptions, hobbies, and toys depending upon your and your child's individual interests.

The point is to get your child interested in how to allocate money into these three areas of wants, needs, and savings so that they can correctly categorize their funds when they are old enough to need to do so.

Chapter 9
Fatherhood in the Modern Age

Fatherhood has been revered as a position of power, protector, and provider since time immemorial. Sometimes, this important role is misunderstood or neglected for its significance in a child's life. At times, it is even reduced to only providing for the general needs of the family and is thought to be exempt from handling emotional or other equally important areas that make a family whole.

Even to a father, the role of being a dad comes with its own complexities that need to be worked with, worked out, or worked around for a father to parent successfully. Fatherhood is a choice you make every day to make the best choices that will help your family thrive. You should also throw in a handful of healthy decisions that will also keep you feeling like more than just a workhorse. You'll need to schedule in some "you-time" and perhaps some time to date your significant other, too, to keep that valuable connection open and well-nourished.

Modern parenthood is quite the intimidating feat. But you should be assured that a father's success is not measured by the number of digits in his bank account or the amount of awards his child has displayed on the refrigerator. Being a successful father today means maintaining an active role in parenting, teaching, caring for, feeding, and engaging with your child to a degree rarely seen in any society prior to the past two decades.

Welcome to fatherhood in a new millennium where you can experience the magic of holding your newborn, gaining unfettered access to their new world. You can be as involved in the care and teaching of your child as you wish your own parents had been. You can make the choice to be there for field trips, bike riding lessons, diaper changes, doctor appointments.

Become the expert on all things that make up and influence your child. You should know if they are up-to-date on all their childhood vaccines. If they are learning new spelling words, you should be there each night to help them practice so they feel prepared to get a good grade on the test at the end of the week.

At each and every opportunity to be a part of your child's life, you should jump in to make that memory with them. There are only 6,570 days of your life, made up of only 18 summers, to spend with your child until they graduate high school and set out to carve their own path. Embrace every moment they invite you to spend with them because it goes too fast.

The Changing Roles and Expectations of Fathers in Today's Society

Way back when humankind became more civilized, settled down, and started the evolution from hunter-gatherer, nomadic living to staying in one area where they could build homes and grow food, men and women raised families in much different ways than we see today. There have always been absent parents, grandparents and extended family members who raise children, and a diverse mix of caregivers who need to ensure that the next generation survives to carry on.

Technology, both a hindrance and a help, has ensured that most adults live well into their 80s so that they can bond with their great and even great great grandchildren. Electronics like smartphones and computers make it possible for families to connect from even thousands of miles away.

If you are stationed overseas for business or for military obligations, it becomes imperative that you check in at home as often as you are allowed. Make the most of these moments. Try to "attend" special events via apps like FaceTime, Skype, Duo, or other video-call platforms. Watch the videos and look at the photos your family shares with you. Your child will notice the effort you make to be present even when you have to be elsewhere.

It is ideal that we can spend every waking moment with our children so that we never miss a single milestone or momentous achievement. These irreplaceable events occur so infrequently that there is usually only a short window of opportunity to enjoy, notice, or capture its unfolding with video or photo-technology so that it may be preserved indefinitely.

Taking pictures is a wonderful way to "freeze" a cherished memory so that you can revisit it with fondness later. Relying only on a mental image or verbal retelling of the event is often not enough. A more tangible reminder like a picture or live-action video assists in dispelling any distress at losing or failing to accurately recall such important milestones in your child's development. You are her most reliable recordkeeper, after all.

When she is older, your daughter will probably turn to you to help her sort through the version of her life, as she recalls it from her perspective. You may remember events differently, and that's okay, but discussing past events with your daughter often will assist in those memories being easier for her to recall later.

There are many other ways that your role as a father would differ from roles of fathers in previous generations than just the increased use of technology. Fathers today generally take on a more hands-on approach to rearing their children. They divide household chores more evenly with their partner. Most fathers try to take time off work to attend their children's school events, plays, concerts, performances, and extracurricular activities.

It's more common to see a father having a heart-to-heart with his daughter in public nowadays than it ever has been before because most men are realizing that they don't want to (and don't have to) miss out of these vital parts of their children's lives just to work all day and come home to a family of strangers who know nothing about him. You can have it all: a family, a career, hobbies, and happiness. Balance is key.

When you notice that your time or attention is focused in a single area of your life for too long, you should shift focus to another area to shake things up a bit. Monotony is not conducive to a happy, healthy, or successful existence. Date your partner. Make time to be silly with your children. Share laughter, your history, and your space with the people you love. Your employer will not notice how many late nights you spend working, or when you choose work over making time to see your child's baseball game. But your child will always notice. Making money isn't the only or even the main goal in life. Money is merely a tool to use to make life easier, to buy food, supplies, entertainment, and essential items.

You'll never be able to buy back the time you'll have missed out on making memories if all you do is work. Take those vacation days, plan special days to focus on being wholly present with your family so that you never need to look back in regret at all the missed chances, missing memories, and empty picture frames that could have held some incredibly epic events that you were there to witness in person. Your daughter will remember.

Balancing Work and Family Life as a Father

Here's the secret to balancing any amount of things, items, ideas, obligations, money, to-dos, and dreams: Enlist more hands. When you can delegate a task to someone else, do it— not for the ones that count like attending your daughter's graduation. But cleaning the house (hire a maid or have your children pitch in), cooking meals (meal-prep the night before is an astounding time-saver or order take-out), and several things work-related can be handled by another employee or it can wait until you return to work the next day.

You can make more money by spending less on perishable items. You can allocate a pot of dirt and seeds on your deck or part of your lawn to grow your own produce to reduce the number of times you run to the store to replace quickly-rotting food. Shop for gently used sneakers instead of splurging on the hottest-trending shoes on social media.

Sure it's not considered "cool" to grow your own food or accept hand-me-downs, but any corners you can cut will help you juggle the ever-encroaching stresses in life that amount to mountains of turmoil that can be avoided by lessening the load here and there whenever you can.

Write down lists of to-dos that need to be completed around the house like repairs, grocery shopping, car maintenance that needs to be done, and bills that need to be paid so that you don't accidentally miss a step and get stressed out that much more.

Schedule time for yourself, and for one-on-one time with your partner, on a family-inclusive calendar that keeps track of each family member's social obligations and appointments. This way, you will know when you need to hire a babysitter or enlist help from extended family members to babysit so that you and your significant other can take a night off together. Emotional maintenance is just as important as getting the oil changed in your vehicle every 2,000 miles. If you don't pop the hood to check the oil level every so often, your car runs dry. It won't get you where you want to go without oil.

Your relationship with your partner is the lifeblood of your family. If your relationship is in shambles, your children will feel that. Their behavior may change; they might act out more often, have problems focusing in school, or fight amongst themselves if they notice something off about how their parents act with each other.

It's challenging to get along with someone "for the kids." A mentality such as this one does not really support your children the way you may have been led to believe. You and your partner will only be passing any dysfunction in your relationship to your child. They will carry that lack of control with them throughout their entire life.

Any relationship they hope to have will be filtered through the lens of how well or how poorly you and any other important caregiver in their childhood were able to work through conflict. You might be passing your heavy burden, short temper, defensiveness, generational trauma, or other hindrance onto your child to carry. If you show others a lack of respect, you risk teaching your child to treat others the same way.

When you can amicably disagree, compromise, and diplomatically address the concerns of someone instead of immediately feeling like you've been attacked, you will start to see a positive change in your household and in yourself. Treat any high-conflict situation as professionally as possible. Only move up the "chain of escalation" matching the other participant's verbal, physical, and emotional if it's absolutely essential to your survival.

Instead, try to move the escalation back down a few notches if you can. Be a calm presence, lower your voice so that the other person needs to lower theirs to hear what you're saying, and embody neutral body language (hands out of pockets, shoulders slouched a bit) to remove any threat. The more professionally you can handle confrontation, the better role model you will be for your child.

The majority of old psychology notions in centuries past (Sigmund Freud's "Oedipus complex", Carl Jung's "mother complex", Alfred Kinsey's "mommy issues") all believed that any dysfunction within an individual was contingent upon if the child's relationship with their mother were healthy, appropriate, affectionate, and attentive. However, modern psychology has shifted this focus to the relationship between a father and their child to be the determining factor in how dysfunctional or well-adjusted a child is as an adult.

If there is chaos within the home, there will be chaos within the child. The best way to remediate any disorder in a child's life is to get control of yourself and let go of trying to control everything else. Life is unpredictable. We can only go along for the ride, trying our best to set small pieces of ourselves in the right order. Too much stress can cause children to shut down, overcompensate, or act out—sometimes, they will perform all three in a single day if they are so distressed that they are unable to regulate, cope, and self-soothe.

To get things back on track, focus on teaching your little one how to calm their nerves by giving them a full-body, extended-length hug. This tight compression of the trunk of the body will signal the brain to release a kind of oxytocin or chemical "love hormone" to help your child relax and kind of "melt" into the safety of your embrace. The National Institute of Health explains this as how "brain oxytocin plays a role in the control of neuroendocrine stress responses by inhibiting the secretion of adrenocorticotropic hormone (ACTH) and thus decreasing the production and release of cortisol" (Li, Hassett, and Seng, 2018). Cortisol is released in the bloodstream along with adrenaline when the fight or flight survival reaction is triggered.

Too much in the bloodstream can cause other normal somatic functions to shut off because the body is unable to allocate all its energy where it should go naturally. A brain under duress is forced to send that energy to the parts of the body that need to function for immediate survival. A child in a constant state of hyperactivity, fear, stress, or uncertainty cannot physically, mentally, cognitively, or emotionally grow to their full potential when they struggle to find security at home.

Under unstable circumstances, like those found previously in hunter-gatherer societies and today in volatile homes, where resources and respite are in short supply, survival mode kicks in for all parties involved. Children, in particular, pay a more impactful price. After all, it is easier to protect a smaller child to find refuge, to carry them away from danger.

In the majority of social constructs worldwide, it is primarily men or patriarchal societies that maintain order and control of others. To not follow the rules set out is to be disobedient, shamed, and punished in some way. A father is seen as the control panel, or motherboard, of the intricate 'computer network' that is his family. When a child feels like their world is chaos, they will grow up always trying to regain that control for themselves.

The cycle of this power struggle will continue to plague the next generation and future relationships if it is left unresolved before your little one leaves the nest. When you approach each day with a more conscientious allocation of your time, attention, and affection then you will begin to notice how it positively affects your household, primarily how it influences your daughter's growth and development.

With you by her side more often than not, your daughter will grow in confidence. It cannot be overstated that you prioritize your daughter as you visualize every way that your actions or inaction could impact how successfully your daughter enters the real world when society labels her an adult at age 18.

Will you have adequately prepared her to persevere or empathize with others who are struggling even if she struggles herself, or will she lose her fighting spirit because no one was there to build her up when she was a little girl who could use more help in her studies? If the bolt comes loose on her night-stand, will you have taught her how to use an allen wrench to tighten it or will she gradually let it fall apart never knowing how to make the repairs on her own?

Even the smallest lessons can become the building blocks, or prerequisites, needed to tackle the more substantial tasks. Using a screwdriver leads to being more proficient with a drill and then your daughter can build her own home with the sturdiness you taught her early on just by you believing she could do what she'd set out to accomplish.

Your presence matters. Your choice of words can build or break. Balance work with how present you are at home more proficiently by tuning out all work-related obligations that call for your attention whenever you're home or supposed to be engrossed in family-time. Refrain from stealing glances at work emails. Keep your phone on silent and only check it if you need reading material in the bathroom.

Be mindful of the amount of time you are spending away from your family. Keep a log if it's brought to your attention that you are being less present when you should be. Do everything within your power to assure the people you love that they matter and that you enjoy spending time with them. You will never be able to replace this missed time.

The Importance of Self-Care and Mental Health for Fathers

On the heels of impressing upon you the importance of making time dedicated to your family, you also need to set aside a specific amount of time to focus on yourself. To heal, to rejuvenate, and restore spent energy weekly or even daily will ensure you are the best version of yourself you can possibly give your family.

What works for you and your family may not work for another father, so be sure to tailor your self-care routine around your schedule and needs. Take up a hobby you enjoy that gets you out of the house and away from work at least once a month.

Take a "me day" at least once each month to get a haircut. Splurge on the pampering aspect of getting a haircut as some barber shops will also trim your facial hair, wash and moisturize your face, and hand you a luxuriously warm towel to place over your freshly shaven face afterward. It feels amazing to have someone take care of your needs, to make you feel exceptional.

Make a dental appointment for yourself twice a year (roughly six months apart) so that you can maintain good dental hygiene. It's absolutely no one's idea of a perfect day to go to the dentist, but it's certainly a necessity to get that tartar build up off your teeth. Brushing, flossing, and using mouthwash at least once a day isn't going to get your teeth as clean as they need to be to deter the formation of cavities. It's only 30 minutes two times a year. You'll leave the dentist's office with smooth teeth and an unworried mind that this is one less thing on your plate.

We discussed the importance of yearly medical checkups for yourself and each of your family members, but dental and eye-care appointments are separate from seeing a medical doctor. It may seem like there are too many appointments to attend between each household member, but they're all necessary in preventing and catching any potential issues that would otherwise be left to get worse without professional intervention.

Give yourself the best start to each day so that you can give your daughter the best years of her life and the best foundation. Nothing is perfect. As long as you're always doing the best you can, that's all anyone can ask of you. You're a human being with very human needs that must be met such as physical exercise, joy, mental stimulation, nourishment, companionship, and rest. If any of those areas are neglected or overindulged, the imbalance can cause tension. Balance is key, as we discussed previously.

To help maintain balance, let your daughter see you engage in activities that you love. Chase your passions. When your child sees you enjoying your work or hobby, it helps normalize her drive to pursue her own dreams and what makes her happy. It provides the formula that will motivate her to chase her passions the way that you did. Your daughter will emulate you. She sees how you handled situations that called on you to be stronger than you knew you were capable of being. Your daughter will use what she knows of how you operate, kept your cool or lost it completely, to guide her along her road to independence.

Every step you take to care for yourself is also a step that takes care of your family.

Conclusion

By this point, you've held your daughter as she took her first breaths and you've walked with her through sleepless nights to keep her safe. You've become a father, a protector, and a role model for this tiny human you helped form. Being the hero your child emulates is no easy task. It can be quite exhausting and leave you scratching your head wondering if you did it right, or what you could have done differently.

This constant questioning is how you know you're doing it right. Only the best parents ponder if they measure up.

Although you'll never truly be certain you've gotten it right or that you've made a difference in your daughter's life, there will be telltale signs that you've done your very best to ensure that your child is loved, nourished, and given all the tools necessary for being successfully independent.

Does she reach for you when she's hurt? Does she run to greet you when you arrive home? Does she look for you in a crowded room or smile at you when she's found you in the sea of parents watching their children perform such adolescent rites of passage like sports, music productions, graduations, and the like? When she's older, does she call you to check in and tell you about what's going on in her life?

If your child reaches out to instigate contact with you in any way, you know that you've been successful as a parent in conveying your love to your child in a way that makes her want to continue with you in her life when your presence is more for her enjoyment than out of necessity for survival. It's time to be proud of your accomplishment because parenthood is not for everyone even though many people become parents.

You are the hero your daughter always knew you were. It's hard work, but the journey is one you'll never forget or substitute for anything else.

Bibliography

Bogle, J. (2021, August 10). *11 ways dads can practice self care and why they should (yes, even you!)*. The Dad. https://www.thedad.com/dads-self-care

Boyd-Barrett, C. (2021, September 27). *When can your baby hear you?*. BabyCenter. https://www.babycenter.com/pregnancy/your-baby/fetal-development-your-babys-hearing_20004866

Brody, J. E. (1981, August 23). *Kinsey study finds homosexuals show early predisposition*. The New York Times. https://www.nytimes.com/1981/08/23/us/kinsey-study-finds-homosexuals-show-early-predisposition.html

Brown, A. (n.d.). *You cannot see your reflection in boiling water*. MindJournal. https://themindsjournal.com/quotes/you-cannot-see-your-reflection-wisdom-quotes

Child Welfare Information Gateway. (2019). *Long-term consequences of child abuse and neglect*. Washington, DC: U.S. Department of Health and Human Services, Administration for Children and Families, Children's Bureau. https://www.childwelfare.gov/pubpdfs/long_term_consequences.pdf

Children or young people who mask or camouflage their needs. (n.d.). Children & Family Health Devon. https://childrenandfamilyhealthdevon.nhs.uk/wp-content/uploads/2020/04/1-minute-guide-masking.pdf

Chun-Hoon, W. (2023, March 14). *5 fast facts: The gender wage gap*. U. S. Department of Labor Blog. https://blog.dol.gov/2023/03/14/5-fast-facts-the-gender-wage-gap

Corpus, J. H., and Good, K. A. (2021). *The effects of praise on children's intrinsic motivation revisited*. In Brummelman, E. (Ed.), *Psychological Perspectives on Praise*. Abington, UK: Routledge. https://www.reed.edu/psychology/motivation/assets/downloads/Corpus_Good_2021.pdf

The criminal justice system: Statistics. (2023). RAINN. https://www.rainn.org/statistics/criminal-justice-system

Definition of domestic violence. (2019). Domestic Abuse Shelter, Inc. https://domesticabuseshelter.org/domestic-violence

Dittmann, M. (2004, June). *Protecting children from advertising*. American Psychological Association. https://apa.org/monitor/jun04/protecting

Dolloff, L. (2006, November 16). *The Oedipus complex*. University of

Bibliography

Vermont. https://www.uvm.edu/~jbailly/courses/tragedy/student%20second%20documents/Oedipus%20Complex.html

Ellis, B. J., Bates, J. E., Dodge, K. A., Fergusson, D. M., Horwood, L. J., Pettit, G. S., and Woodward, L. (2003, May 16). *Does father absence place daughters at special risk for early sexual activity and teenage pregnancy?*. Child Development. https://srcd.onlinelibrary.wiley.com/doi/abs/10.1111/1467-8624.00569

Garey, J. (2023, February 4). *13 ways to boost your daughter's self-esteem.* Child Mind Institute. https://childmind.org/article/13-ways-to-boost-your-daughters-self-esteem

Janvrin, R. (2023, March 7). *NBA vs WNBA: Revenue, salaries, viewership, attendance and ratings.* WSN. https://www.wsn.com/nba/nba-vs-wnba

Li, Y., Hassett, A. L., & Seng, J. S. (2018, November 20). *Exploring the mutual regulation between oxytocin and cortisol as a marker of resilience.* Arch Psychiatr Nurs. 2019 Apr;33(2):164-173. https://www.ncbi.nlm.nih.gov/pmc/articles/PMC6442937/

Malman, S. J. (2022, February 22). *Who causes more car accidents: Men or women?.* Malman Law. https://www.malmanlaw.com/malman-law-injury-blog/who-causes-more-car-accidents-men-or-women/

Menstrual Cycle. (2022, December 9). Cleveland Clinic. https://my.clevelandclinic.org/health/articles/10132-menstrual-cycle

Nag, O. S. (2019, August 2). *The Khasi people of Meghalaya: Where women rule.* Land Portal. https://landportal.org/node/91997

Plowman, V. (2018, August 6). *The positive impact a father has on his daughter.* Today Parenting Team. https://community.today.com/parentingteam/post/the-positive-impact-a-father-has-on-his-daughter

Poole, N. (2023). *8 ways to model a healthy relationship for your children.* Kiddipedia. https://kiddipedia.com.au/8-ways-to-model-a-healthy-relationship-to-your-children/

Praise, encouragement, and rewards. (2020, August 31). Raising Children Network Australia. https://raisingchildren.net.au/toddlers/connecting-communicating/connecting/

Purrington, M. (2020, October 21). *Carl Jung on the "mother complex".* Carl Jung Depth Psychology. https://carljungdepthpsychologysite.blog/2020/10/21/carl-jung-on-the-mother-complex

Quick facts about sexual assault in America—2023. (2022, May 25). PlanStreet. https://www.planstreetinc.com/quick-facts-about-sexual-assault-in-america

Quinn, K., Eisner, L., and Ross, G. (2022). Cursive [Song]. On *Happy Never After*. VOILA.

Rapson, J. (n.d.). *Powerful Dove ad exposes how social media beauty is harming our girls*. Her View From Home. https://herviewfromhome.-com/dove-ad-social-media-beauty

Reilly, K. C. (2021, June 20). *The power of a girl dad*. Newsweek. https://www.newsweek.com/power-girl-dad-opinion-1596063

Rishikof, J. (n.d.). *How a father's aggression can impact their daughter's development (and what to do about it)*. Dads of Daughters. https://ihaveadaughter.com/how-a-fathers-aggression-can-impact-their-daughters-development/

Rogers, E. (2021, April 19). *Why Dove's real beauty campaign was so successful*. Live Oak Communications. https://www.liveoakcommunications.com/post/why-dove-s-real-beauty-campaign-was-so-successful

Sex education and talking with children about sex: 0-8 years. (2022, April 11). Raising Children Network Australia. https://raisingchildren.net.au/school-age/development/sexual-development/sex-education-children

Shu, J. (2021, April 28). *When can my unborn baby hear me? I'd love to be able to read and sing to them*. American Academy of Pediatrics. https://www.healthychildren.org/English/tips-tools/ask-the-pediatrician/Pages/I%E2%80%99m-pregnant-and-would-like-to-sing-to-my-unborn-baby.aspx

Swift, T. (2022). You're losing me [Song]. On *Midnights*. Republic Records.

The Unearth Women Team. (2023, March 22). *5 matriarchal societies where women are in charge*. Unearth Women. https://www.unearthwomen.com/5-matriarchal-societies-where-women-are-in-charge/

Wisner, W. (2021, November 1). *The best time for talking to teens is at night—here's why*. Your Teen Magazine. https://yourteenmag.com/family-life/communication/best-time-talking-to-teens

Made in the USA
Columbia, SC
12 November 2024

46312677R00070